How

How We Met

Real-Life

Tales of

How Happily

Married Couples

Found Each Other

—❤—

Michelle Bowers &

Melissa Steinfeld Galett

ST. MARTIN'S GRIFFIN ❧ NEW YORK

Book design by Michelle McMillian

ISBN 0-312-24303-0

First St. Martin's Griffin Edition: February 2000

10 9 8 7 6 5 4 3 2 1

Acknowledgments

♥

We're immensely grateful for all the help we received on our project. Many thanks to:

All the couples we interviewed, and everyone who passed us along to a friend, relative, or coworker with a great story. Without all of you, there would be no book.

Bret Watson and Sarah Woodson, for being devoted proofreaders and cheerleaders. You kept us inspired.

Richard Marks, for planting the seed.

Richard Mintzer, for being so helpful by sharing his contacts and advice.

Our agent, Sheree Bykofsky, for putting our work into the right hands.

Our editor, Marian Lizzi, for bringing our idea to life.

And lastly, our husbands, Jarvis Bowers and Lawrence Galett, for giving us our own happy endings.

Introduction

♥

It is the happiest of events: the moment a special person wanders into your life and changes everything that is to follow—the day you meet your spouse. Two people collide full force and become each other's destiny. What makes it so magical is that it is so utterly uncontrollable and unpredictable. What if you hadn't gone to the movies that afternoon? You would never have been buying popcorn at just the same moment he was ordering his Coke. What if you hadn't gone out with your friend that Saturday evening? You never would have met her on the dance floor. Or if you'd turned left instead of right? Who knows what you would have missed, how your life would have been lacking without that fateful encounter.

These moments are so special and life defining that they become stories couples tell over and over again. It's usually the first question people ask a twosome: "So, how did you two meet?" The desire to know the intimate details that united a happy pair is partly rooted in voyeurism. *Was there an immediate spark between them? What was it about this random meeting that produced a lifetime match?* And sometimes single friends pose the question for educational purposes. *Oh, jogging in Golden Gate Park, eh? I've got to hang out there more often.*

One common thread that has emerged from years of listening to happy mates talk about how they met is that there is never any way to anticipate the big moment. The meeting could happen at jury duty, in the 7-Eleven, or while waiting tables. You just never know. We heard from others who turned their computer terminals into a direct pipeline to love. Chat rooms, on-line personal ads, and E-mails between friends have all yielded a bumper crop of electronic-turned-real-life love affairs. And don't forget about the short kid from tenth grade math class. Sometimes love strikes when former classmates meet again many years after graduation—at weddings or reunions or flea markets. Wherever the meeting, whatever the circumstances, at least one person has to take a little risk. Whether it's asking for a phone number, a date, or even just offering a smile from across the room, putting oneself on the line is what makes everything else possible. First encounters, whether they seem momentous or entirely forgettable at the time, can take two people on a long journey together—one that leads all the way to the altar.

There are, of course, some early, unmistakable signs of good things to come. Dozens of happily marrieds talked about how they knew it was right because they felt so utterly comfortable in the other's presence. It's a feeling that just can't be faked. There are no awkward silences, no uncomfortable moments. You might even feel like best friends, even though you met only hours earlier. One woman even fell asleep in her date's apartment while he was cooking her dinner for the first time. This may not be the steamy stuff romance novels are made of, but it certainly was a good sign. Most couples know it's right when they don't have to try to make it work, when it just does, effortlessly. Another woman spoke of how she lived in the moment and when it came to men, refused to agonize, analyze, or anticipate. When romance just happens naturally, it's able to bloom spectacularly.

Most important, a future spouse has got to be able to hold up his or her end of the conversation. If there's no talk, there's no relationship, either. As a wise person once said, "Marry for conversation, because everything else fades away."

Several years ago, my partner Melissa and I decided that love stories about how couples found their way to each other was a topic well worthy of a book of its own. Melissa, who in her single days admitted to being preoccupied with meeting The One, has spent years asking married couples how they met. One day Melissa asked me her infamous question about my husband and me. Shameless romantics, Melissa and I launched into a frenzy of storytelling. We knew we weren't alone in our curiosity about the creation of lasting couples.

We began by asking every married couple we know how they met each other. In our search for good stories, we spread the word of our project on the Internet, at work, and at exercise class. No one—not even a random passenger sitting next to Melissa on a plane—was safe from our probing and prying. What follows is a collection of our favorites out of the dozens upon dozens of tales that we've heard over the last few years. Just a few of the names have been changed, but all the stories are entirely true. (Each name that appears first is of the person who's telling the story.)

Appropriately enough, during our work on this project, Melissa met her husband. Maybe just thinking about all these love connections put her in the right frame of mind. Or maybe it was just that she happened to be on a Manhattan sidewalk at exactly the right moment. One day as she was leisurely strolling down East Seventy-first Street, doing a little window shopping on the way home from work, she asked a passerby for the time. This handsome man got right to flirting with her, and they fell in step together while walking down the street. Engrossed in conversation, Melissa strolled right past her apartment, and they ended up sitting on a park bench contentedly chatting away. Moments later Lawrence asked Melissa for her phone number and a kiss. She said yes to the number, an adamant "No!" to the smooch. Months later, he asked her for something else: her hand in marriage. For Melissa, a little thing like forgetting her watch one day led to the most important turning point in her life. What's even more astounding is that Melissa's sister also met her husband while walking down the street in New York City. Andrea's story is on page 69.) To this day, the sisters talk about how incredibly lucky they were to stumble across their soulmates on bustling city sidewalks.

As for my own tale, it amuses my husband, Jarvis, and me greatly that we have two wildly different versions of the event. Here's mine. I was at a party in Manhattan that my friend Suzie brought me to on the spur of the moment. Halfway through the night, Suzie pointed out my future husband, who was parked at the food table by himself. "Check out that interesting-looking guy!" she said of this six-foot-four bald man who has creamy smooth skin the color of coffee. *Hmm, interesting,* I agreed, and thought nothing more of it.

Later, we introduced ourselves, and after the entire group relocated to a local bar, Jarvis asked me to buy him a beer or two.

(He had no cash, was his excuse.) I believe there may have been some dancing involved, definitely a back rub (of which I was the lucky recipient), and a lot of showing off at the pool table on his part. At 4:00 A.M. Jarvis thought he'd lure me back to his place with the tempting offer of "playing darts." Not only was it one of the worst lines I'd ever heard, but he called me by the wrong name when he asked me for a kiss! Still, feeling extremely charitable, I suppose, I wrote my phone number in lip pencil on his *Wall Street Journal*, and by the next morning, my phone was ringing.

Jarvis has brought so much to my life, most of all a sense of wonder and gratitude that this giving and sensitive man—who has seen even the worst parts of me—truly cherishes me. He showed me for the first time what a healthy, fulfilling relationship was all about. We bring out the best in each other. Very early on, a voice inside me told me confidently that Jarvis was my partner for life, my match, and my mate. The best part about the way we got together is that it wasn't hard work. There were no Big Talks, no fighting. (Well, just a little, maybe.) It was simply easy, natural, and uncomplicated from the very first. There was one other important thing, too: he makes a great banana bread. Even now I think about how easily we could have passed each other by, without even knowing what we were missing. How different my life would be now if I hadn't gone to the party that cold November night.

—Michelle Bowers
Los Angeles, June 1999

How We Met

Bill and Nancy

oral surgeon, 60; internist, 48

married May 17, 1998

♥

I was at a point in my life when I knew I wanted to get married. Finding the right woman, though, was taking a lot longer than I'd hoped. One Sunday afternoon in March 1997, I took a date to a performance of the Westchester Philharmonic. During the intermission, as we were talking in the lobby, I spotted this stunning woman. I loved the way she looked; I loved her posture, her smile. I loved the way she related to her friends. Her eyes were so alive, so bright, and so happy. I said to myself, *What an attitude.* I mean, she was just terrific. As she walked away, I thought, *Wow. That's her. This is who I've been looking for.* It was purely a one-way meeting. She never even saw me.

This woman was contrary to everything I always thought I was looking for. I'm six foot four, and I always liked very tall, blond women. Here I was, suddenly bowled over by a petite brunette. I desperately wanted to talk to her, but I'm a gentleman and it certainly would have been rude to my date that evening. Then I remembered: there was another concert five weeks later. I decided then and there that I would come to that concert alone and hope she would be there. I would introduce myself then.

After intermission, my date and I returned to our seats, and I spied the woman from the lobby sitting in the orchestra section. I thought to myself immediately, *If I know what seat she's in, I might be able to track her down.* Telling my date my beeper had gone off, I excused myself to go call my office—an unabashed lie: I ran downstairs and looked at which row and seat she was in.

In the office on Monday, I couldn't stop thinking about her. I just couldn't wait until the next concert so many weeks away. *And what if she wasn't a subscription member of the Philharmonic?* I had better write to her, I decided. I couldn't just let this go. In a two-page letter, I described what I liked about her and told her all about myself—my background and family. Just to be safe, I also mentioned that I was much younger than the average gray-haired concertgoer at the Philharmonic. I ended by asking her to call me if she liked. On the front of the envelope I wrote, "To the Woman in Seat L6." And I sent it off with a note to the Philharmonic public relations director asking her if she could forward this letter to the woman who held the ticket for that seat, assuming it didn't breach any rules. I learned a long, long time ago that the meek shall not inherit the earth—you have to go for it.

A few weeks passed and I didn't hear anything from the Philharmonic or the woman in Seat L6. One Sunday, I was at home with a friend when my phone rang. I decided not to answer it, figuring if it was important enough, the person would leave a message on my machine. An hour later, the phone rang again. When my friend finally left, I rushed back into the house to try to figure out who had been ringing me every hour for the last three hours. But no one left any messages! I had never tried this before, but I picked up the phone and dialed *69. An unfamiliar woman answered and I asked, "Who is this?" She said to me, "What do you mean, 'who's this'? You called me!" And I replied, "Well, this is Bill. I'm returning your call. I dialed star-six-nine." Then she uttered the three most beautiful words, "This is L6!"

Her name was Nancy. That day at the concert, she had been a guest of her friend, Paula who owned the season tickets. My letter made its way to Paula, who realized it was meant for Nancy. We spoke on the phone for a while that day and I learned she was a doctor, too. The fact that she was still a total stranger didn't stop me from being nuts about her. There was another concert coming up the following week, and I suggested we go together. She thought that was a wonderful idea.

Before the concert, I took her to a lovely restaurant, and we enjoyed a chilled bottle of white wine. During the meal, she was a little questioning but receptive to me. Nancy is a person who believes that everything happens for a reason and that there are no coincidences. This woman has such a positive attitude. To her, there is nothing bad in the world. I was ecstatic just being around her. I knew that day that this gal was the one. I felt it in my bones, and I was starting to get nervous a little. How could this be real?

We had a wonderful lunch and it was a gorgeous afternoon. I took the top down on my car, and we drove up to the concert hall for the performance. Afterward, we took a beautiful long nature walk in a nearby park. That's where I held her hand for the first time. As the sun started to go down, I said to her, "Well, we have to have dinner now."

When I put her back in her car, I kissed her on the cheek good-bye, and I told her I would speak to her very shortly. I called her as soon as she got home. After we hung up, I phoned my son, who is my best friend. "Jonathan," I said. "I just met your future stepmother." He admonished, "Dad, get with it! Come back to earth. What have you been drinking?" I said, "I'm telling you—I am absolutely in love."

Nancy has brought such an infusion of life into my world. In the years I've known her, she has never uttered a negative word about anything. I love her positive attitude about everything. And you don't even need to talk to her to realize this—it just spills over into every facet of who she is. From the moment I met her, a song kept playing over and over in my head. The lyrics are, "I hear singing and there's no one there, I smell blossoms and the trees are bare." It described my feelings for her exactly.

Later that year, I took Nancy to Bermuda. Our very first night there, we were sitting at dinner in a beautiful, scenic restaurant and suddenly I knew I had to ask her to marry me. That was *the* moment—ring or no ring. I hadn't planned it or debated over the decision to propose. I just did it.

We were married on the stage of the Westchester Philharmonic. The setting was beautiful and perfect for a wedding. We gathered under a very sentimental huppa that Nancy's grandfather had sewn with patches of fabric from the old country. Our friends and relatives held up the huppa while my daughters and son—who was my best man—and Nancy's brothers stood up as our witnesses. We recited our vows while all our guests looked on from the audience. Most importantly, we had a spotlight shining on seat L6. In the middle of the ceremony the rabbi said, "Everybody turn around. That's where she was." Exactly where I found her.

Jim and Pam

real estate executive, 34; pharmaceutical salesperson, 29
married December 27, 1997

♥

We tell everyone this story. I was coming home from work really late one night wearing a rumpled suit and a loosened tie. I was an exhausted bachelor and I needed to eat. So where else would I go but the 7-Eleven? In the store I took a turn down the candy aisle and I saw this really cute girl. We gave each other dumbfounded, lingering glances. I looked at her like, *Wow. She's cute.* She looked at me like she might be thinking I was pretty cute, too.

Pam was wearing messy housework clothes and had paint in her hair and no makeup on at all. She was carrying a bunch of plates and cups so I asked her, "Hey, where's the party?" I mean, I had to say something. She told me her parents were helping her paint her condo and she was just picking up Chinese food and some soft drinks for them. I asked, "And are you bringing that stuff back for your husband or your boyfriend?" I wasn't wasting any time, here. Luckily, the answer was neither. Coincidentally, I ran into her again at the checkout counter and we talked some more. I was finished paying before she was, so I shuffled out of the store as slowly as possible, hoping she'd catch up to me, which she did.

We talked for a while out in the parking lot. Then she was about to leave and I said, "Well, maybe I'll run into you again sometime." But Los Angeles is a big city, and all of a sudden I realized I might never see her again. I couldn't let her leave, so I walked back up to her and—desperate for something to say— asked if she went to UCLA. It was a weed-out question, to figure out how old she was. Thankfully, she wasn't a young undergrad, so I took a huge leap and asked her for her phone number. I had to; I just couldn't let her drive away. I think by then she could tell I wasn't a freak or anything. And she didn't hesitate—she just whipped her pen right out. I went home after that and told my dad that I just met this great girl and I thought I was going to marry her. It was love at first sight.

It was a Friday when I first called and asked her out. She was busy for Saturday but suggested we go out that very same night. I liked her spontaneity. We went to a movie and then I bought her an ice cream. It was a nice low-pressure night, especially since we didn't know each other at all and, aside from one convenience-store encounter, had nothing in common yet.

The next weekend everything fell into place. I took Pam out Friday night, Saturday, Saturday night, and then we went to church together Sunday morning. We didn't plan to spend the whole weekend together, it just happened. Wondering if I seemed too available never even entered into the equation because it all just felt so right. It was an immediate lock. And from then on, we were a couple. Even that second weekend, I knew that we would definitely be together for a while. I didn't know if my marriage premonition would come true or not, but Pam and I were going to be serious.

I decided not to tell Pam about my early thoughts of marriage until it was exactly the right time. A year and a half later, I proposed to her by saying, "The first day we met, I told my dad I knew I was going to marry you. Tonight I'd like to make that a reality." Pam made my dream come true. She said yes.

Doug and Kathryn

technical writer, 55; homemaker, 52

married September 4, 1967

♥

Ours was a whirlwind, wartime romance. The Vietnam War was raging, and I got drafted. Willing to do anything to stay out of the army, I signed up for the navy and shipped off to Japan, near Yokohama. I was only twenty-one.

My buddies and I were going downtown one day to get off the base and blow off some steam. We didn't have a lot of money, so the best we could hope for was finding a bar and some cheap beer. There was a bus that took us right from the base into Yokohama, but as we went to catch it, we saw the tailpipe disappearing around the corner. If we had only been a minute earlier! Being dirt poor, we couldn't afford to take a cab. Out of desperation, we decided to check out what was going on at the base instead.

That late August day, the base happened to be hosting a local Japanese harvest festival, Bon Adori, which was in full swing by the time we arrived. Having nothing better to do, we watched the dancing and the fireworks and tossed back a few Japanese beers. Standing up against a fence, one of my buddies started talking to the girl next to him. I wasn't interested in her initially. She was American, and dating Japanese girls was much more fun and intriguing for us military boys. Plus, she was a navy brat— her Dad was a "lifer"—and I hated the navy. I didn't really want to have anything to do with this girl, Kathryn. But then my friend wandered away, leaving me standing right next to her. When we started talking, I discovered I was able to talk to her easily and we got along quite well. She was really pretty cute! I boxed my other friend Woody out before he had a chance to move in on Kathryn.

She had been in Japan with her parents for a few months but hadn't seen any sights. I volunteered to show her around. We loved to go to Tokyo and sit in coffeehouses and listen to classical music. I took Kathryn on her first trip on a subway. She'd never been on one before. It was so much fun, and she was such an interesting traveling companion. We walked our feet off in Japan.

When I talked to Kathryn, I never felt awkward. I could tell her about all the things that interested me, and she listened. She was able to do the same, and we found out that we liked many of the same things. And she would laugh at my feeble jokes. Kathryn had a nice laugh—she still does. She complemented me, and I like to think I complemented her.

We also discovered that we both had Norwegian ancestors and that our families came from the same region in Norway, no more than one hundred miles apart. We like to think that had we not met in Japan, maybe we would have found each other in Norway. . . .

After just a little while, I was hooked on her. It took me only four months to propose. (Hey, it was wartime.) We married almost exactly one year after we met. Woody, who missed the bus with me that day on the base, was my best man. At our wedding he was introduced to Kathryn's sister and *they* later fell in love and got married! That one missed bus ride resulted in two very happy unions. There isn't a day that's gone by that I've taken that for granted. Thank God I missed the bus.

Jane and Matthew

advertising executive, 34; lawyer, 32

married October 18, 1992

♥

When my best friend from childhood asked me to be her maid of honor, there was just one condition: she didn't want me to bring a date to the wedding. Laurie was marrying an English man, Jonathan, and they both desperately wanted me to meet Matthew, Jonathan's brother and best man. The only thing I had ever heard about him was that at a New Year's Eve party once they all danced the lambada, and Matthew danced with an air mattress.

He irritated me from the very first. When I met him I mentioned that I lived in Germany for a year. He asked if I spoke German and said, "If you're like most Americans you probably know how to ask where the train station is." I replied, *"Fick mal ab."* Let's just say I strongly insulted him.

Even though Matthew really got on my nerves, there was something about him that I thought was very funny. Annoying in a funny way. He had the English superiority thing going on, and we teased each other constantly with a competition of words. There's something about English humor: they love to malign each other. It's very clever and amusing, but if you're not used to it, it can be very biting. I was definitely struck by him.

The week after Laurie and Jonathan's wedding, Matthew went to Cape Cod with his family for the Fourth of July weekend. I was also going to the Cape to visit some friends. Matthew and I made plans to get together one afternoon. When I arrived at the inn where he was staying, Matthew observed, "Two hours is a very long way to drive to see someone you don't know very well." I was infuriated that he had embarrassed me in front of his family. All during the drive home I thought, *This guy is really too much.* When he called the next day to ask me to dinner, I barked, "I don't want to spend any time with you! I have better things to do with my life than listen to you insult me!" I ranted for a while before I hung up. My sister told me I was a little harsh. So I called him back eating humble pie and agreed to go out to dinner.

That night Matthew brought me a lily plant and a bottle of champagne, on which he had written a funny poem. He felt bad about having given me such a hard time. That's when I thought, *This guy is really sweet.* And that night at dinner my fortune cookie read, prophetically, "You will take a trip across the ocean."

We kissed that night, which was a big moment. And then he left the next day for England. We wrote letters and he sent me flowers one day, which just happened to be my birthday.

A few months later, some friends of mine asked me to come visit them in England, and I jumped at the idea. Pretending I was going on holiday to see them, I called Matthew, and with one of my more pathetic lines I said, "I'm going to be in London and I wanted to know if you wanted to get some coffee." He graciously replied, "Coffee and perhaps a meal?" I had already booked the trip, so I told him the dates and he stammered, "Um . . . well, I'm going to have to see, yes, well, let me see if I can do some juggling." I immediately knew there was another girl.

On the plane over it really struck me. *What am I doing?!* When I got to Heathrow Airport he was waiting for me wearing a fedora and a trench coat. I had told him I loved tea and these special English biscuits, and he had brought me a whole case of them, along with a thermos of hot tea. I was amazed that he remembered and thought it was the cutest thing.

We spent the week together before I traveled up north to York to see my friends. Two days after I left London, Matthew showed up unannounced in York. Along with him, he brought Maria, a girl who was visiting him from Spain. I don't know if Maria knew who I was, but I realized pretty quickly that she was the "other woman"! She was originally supposed to go to London the week I was there, but he bumped her off a week because of me. I felt kind of bad for her that she was tagging along as Matthew was chasing after me, and it was a little weird and awkward. He was just dying to see me, I guess, and had to find me. I was touched that he wanted to be with me again.

When I got back to London, Matthew drove me to the airport. It was all very dramatic and sad. We didn't know when we would see each other again. Eleven or twelve visits later, he wrote a letter to my parents, which they opened as a Christmas present. "I can't think of any better gift than your daughter," Matthew wrote. He was asking for their permission to marry me. They all took me to the airport on Christmas day and sent me off to London to get engaged.

Laurie and Jonathan hadn't said anything to us this entire time; they were afraid to curse it. By the time we got engaged we weren't even sure if they'd be happy. But when we called from London to tell them the news, they just screamed with joy.

Danette and Kevin

software salesperson, 37; general manager, 41

married October 24, 1998

♥

Kevin and I lived on the same street, just ten houses apart, in a suburb of Atlanta. We had the exact same house and we each had two kids. I'd been living there four years, and he'd been there two. Our children were all friends and played together in the neighborhood. I knew his kids and he knew mine. But in all this time, we had never met.

One morning in September, the kids were going back to school, and Kevin and I were both at the bus stop at the same time. I had seen him before in the neighborhood, driving his car. But I had no idea he was single. One of my neighbors had actually told me he was married. But he'd been divorced for a few years. I was, too, and wasn't interested in dating anybody. I just wasn't looking.

That morning, we happened to notice each other. We talked

about getting the kids off to school and how hard it was being a single parent. That investigative conversation quickly established that we were both unattached. Somehow we discovered we both liked sushi, and I mentioned how hard it is to find someone to have sushi with because a lot of people hate it. He suggested we go together sometime. I honestly didn't even consider it a date.

Aside from being really cute, he had a great smile. This man was very laid back and calm. I could just tell Kevin was easygoing and lots of fun. It was obvious that his kids just adored him—even my son did. This is how I describe my husband now: he's comfortable with himself. And that's very important no matter where you are. Whatever we did, even if I took him to a party where he knew not a soul, he'd be off socializing the whole night. He always has something in common with everybody. That first day at the bus stop, he made me feel very comfortable and at ease.

It took us about two weeks to set the night for our sushi outing. Meanwhile I was seeing him every morning at 7:00 at the bus stop. I wasn't putting on makeup for the trip down the block. Having just gotten out of bed, I was usually barefoot and in a big T-shirt, with my hair pulled back. I don't even know if I brushed my teeth. Kevin was always dressed up in a suit because he'd be on his way to work. It was really funny—I thought, *If he can ask me out at seven in the morning looking like this, I've got nothing to worry about.*

Our first evening together, we went to dinner and to a few bars afterward to listen to jazz. It was so casual and easy, like spending time with my best friend. I felt as if I had known him for a hundred years and there was nothing I was afraid to tell him. We had a very pleasant, comfortable night. I was definitely attracted to Kevin. But the thought just never crossed my mind that this could be something significant. I just thought it was a night out with a friend.

As we were driving home that night, I suddenly realized that this was a date. The next logical thought was that he might try to kiss me good night. Sheer panic set in. I had had a few dates since my divorce, but there had been nothing physical. With Kevin, I thought kissing might not be such a bad idea, but I didn't know if I could deal with it. If he had slowed down the car, I might seriously have jumped out.

We had left all four kids with baby-sitters at my house, so when we returned home, Kevin came inside to collect his children. As we walked in, he backed me up toward a wall and leaned over to kiss me. I just froze. I didn't move a lip, a hand, a muscle. But he kissed me anyway. I felt like the biggest idiot and was so embarrassed. I thought I had blown this forever. To try to salvage the moment, I cracked a lame joke. He, of course, assumed I didn't kiss him because I wasn't interested.

To my surprise, he called me the next day and asked for a second date. At lunch the following week, I apologized for the kissing incident. "I'm so embarrassed," I told him. "I don't know what happened." He felt bad because he hadn't meant to make me nervous. Then he asked, "Do you think we could work on those kisses?" Flirtatiously, I replied, "I think we could do that. I swear I get better." After lunch, he walked me to my car, which was right in front of his office building. He opened my car door for me and planted kiss number two on me. Again, I was surprised.

I knew for sure that I was meant to be with Kevin when he showed up one night at my house for dinner and I was sitting in front of the TV glued to the Georgia-Florida football game. I had completely forgotten to get ready for our date. It was tied in the third quarter and I couldn't pull myself away from the TV, but Kevin didn't care. Nothing was ever very complicated with us. Things just always worked out. Kevin later told me that a few months before we met at the bus stop around the neighborhood he noticed me. I was washing my car in my driveway, covered in soap and scrubbing away. He says that's when he fell in love with me.

Our kids were so excited when we told them we were getting married. We had our wedding in the mountains, and the four children were up on the altar with us. They were our entire wedding party.

Before we met, Kevin didn't think there would ever be another relationship for him. It was all just too painful. And when you're not looking, that's when it happens. We were instant soul mates, instant best friends. What were the odds of us finding each other?

Mark and Lesia

advertising salesman, 40; registered nurse, 43

married July 31, 1982

♥

I remember the first time I saw her: it was the day she started working at McDonald's, and she was in the back of the store with one of the managers for her training. I saw her across the room and I remember being stunned—as stunned as a 17-year-old can get. I was totally knocked out by her figure and her long blond hair. She was a vision in her blue polyester uniform: pants and a smock and a goofy little beret. Wow!

I had been working at McDonald's in a small town outside of Cincinnati for a year when Lesia began working there in the summer of '76. She was twenty and going to a local college to study nursing.

It took me three weeks to ask Lesia out. We really didn't know each other very well at all. One night, a coworker of mine dared me to ask Lesia on a date. So I did. Lesia laughed and said, "Oh yeah, sure. Pick me up at seven-thirty." She was totally shocked when I showed up. She thought I was just joking around and it was never going to happen. I was thinking the same thing—there was no way she was going to be home and actually go out with me.

We went to a movie that night and saw *Obsession* with Clint Roberts. I don't know why I remember that, I just always have. Afterward, we went to Pizza Hut, the competitor! Of course, I got real cute and played "Feel Like Making Love" on the jukebox. Lesia gave me the evil eye the whole time the song played. It didn't go over well—not at all.

With Lesia and me, it was instant chemistry. She was extremely honest, and there wasn't any of the kind of giggly, silly "Do you like me?" stuff. Not that I was overly mature or anything.

McDonald's wasn't exactly the most romantic backdrop for falling in love. We made out behind the Dumpsters in the parking lot or met in the back of the store and kissed while we were getting napkins. We were covered with oil and food all the time, and the store was smelly and greasy. This was also twenty years ago, so we all had to wear hair nets, silly paper hats, and uniforms that would probably melt if we got too close to the grill. In the midst of all of that, who would have thought I'd stumble across my future wife?

What I loved about Lesia—and still do—is her loyalty. If I had problems with my parents or teenage growing pains, she was always my biggest fan. That's a lot of what kept us together all those years. I knew that no matter what, I could trust her to help me and trust her to be honest with me. Her sincerity is a big part of who she is.

For a while, we'd go back to McDonald's on our anniversary for hamburgers and shakes. We don't eat fast food on a regular basis anymore. But whenever we do, it's McDonald's or nothing. There's no Jack-in-the-Box in our house!

John and Alessandra

marketing manager, 43; hotel executive, 33

married April 1, 1990

♥

She smiled at me. That's how it began. This dark Italian beauty was on the cable car along with me. I was working in Munich during the summer of '87, and a friend and I drove down to Salzburg for dinner one night. After we ate, we searched for this wonderful castle we had heard about. We drove right past it once, but suddenly, we did a U-turn and found ourselves staring right at it. It was a spectacular sight.

In order to get up to the top of the steep hill, where the castle was perched, we rode up in a little tram, called a *fonicolare*. It was there that I first caught sight of her. She was talking to her friend and what hit me were her striking eyes and her smile—directed at me! I smiled right back and thought to myself, *Here's another girl I'll never meet....*

My friend and I wandered around the castle, which offered the most breathtaking views of Salzburg. But as we were seeing the sights, I followed this beautiful girl and her friend, trying desperately to think of some way I could meet them. Any and all bright ideas, however, eluded me. Maybe I could listen in to their conversation and just butt in, I thought. But they weren't even speaking English. And what do you say to someone you don't know?

I wasn't giving up. I wanted desperately to meet her. And my friend was not helping, saying, "Forget it, you don't even know her." Because I was doggedly pursuing this girl, my friend and I missed a concert that was taking place in the castle. To top it all off, I suddenly realized I had lost her. We searched around but couldn't find her anywhere. Now my friend was really mad at me. Finally he suggested we leave and go get a cup of coffee.

Back at the *fonicolare*, I was so disappointed that I had squandered my opportunity to meet this girl. All of a sudden, there she was. I just smiled.

There was a long string of unusual coincidences that just didn't stop. And every little thing was an unlikely event—if we had found the castle when we were looking for it the first time, I wouldn't have seen her on the *fonicolare*. Once we were in the castle, if they hadn't gotten lost while we were looking for them, we all wouldn't have ended up back at the *fonicolare* at the same time, as we did.

On the way down the hill, I asked her if she spoke English. A little bit, she said. That meant *very* little. Her name was Alessandra and she was from Italy. Luckily my friend spoke Italian. So *he* was having a conversation with her. I didn't have any idea what they were saying, and I was getting a little annoyed. Alessandra was paying no attention to me. I felt like a little kid—I tugged on my pal's shirttails and said, "Ask her if she wants to go out with me!" We all went to a little café for dessert and were getting along very well, but they were staying at a youth hostel with an 11:00 p.m. curfew and had to run off. The last thing I wanted her to do was disappear into the city, so we offered to give them a ride. Looking back, they easily could have said no, and I never would have seen her again. But they made a quick judgment call about us and decided we were okay.

We got lost on the way and the girls forgot which hostel they were staying in, but we got them back by 10:59. After a fun night, we all said good-bye. But there was nothing promising about it. It didn't make any sense for me to pursue Alessandra.

The next day, back at work in Munich, I couldn't stop thinking about the Italian girl in Salzburg. I had to see her again. My friend let me take the car, but as I drove off to find Alessandra, he stood there shaking his head, thinking I was nuts. Drive four hours to try to track down some girl wandering around in a big city? It was ridiculous.

Manning the front desk at the hostel was a gorgeous blond Austrian girl. When I asked about Alessandra, she told me she had gone out for the evening. She was *quite* sure. Then, with a sultry look, she winked and asked me, "What you do now?" It was so blatant that I thought I was dreaming! I must admit she gave me a moment of hesitation. Just then, at that exact moment, in walked Alessandra. She ran up and gave me a hug. The girl at the desk was very embarrassed. If I'd arrived even ten minutes earlier, I never would have found Alessandra. And if Alessandra had walked in a few minutes *later*, she might have caught me in an embarrassing situation with the Austrian girl. Our timing was perfect.

I drove four hours to see Alessandra every night that week. I just couldn't stay away from her. I was getting back in at three or four in the morning, and by the end of the week I was pretty ragged. I was so tired I was practically falling asleep at work.

At the end of the week, the girls came back with me to Munich, which was the next stop on their itinerary. After Munich, they told me they were heading to Vienna. "Vienna!" I said. "I'll go with you. I've always wanted to go there!" This couldn't have been further from the truth. The only thing I knew about that city was that it was Freud's hometown. The only problem was that I had to go to Frankfurt on business, so I asked them to wait for me before they left for Vienna. They couldn't because they were running out of money and vacation time. "Okay," I said, "I'll find you in Vienna when I'm back from my business trip."

"How are you going to do that?" Alessandra asked wisely. Confidently, I replied, "I found you in Salzburg, I'll find you in Vienna."

I was a young American guy, having fun in my spare time in Europe, and this romance seemed like such a ridiculous proposition. I shouldn't have been feeling that this was the start of some great relationship, because it couldn't be. My rational mind was saying: don't get involved, it's just fun. At the same time, Alessandra wasn't someone I could be practical about. The litmus test would be Vienna. If I was truly interested, I'd find her there, somehow.

After my business trip, I decided to fly to Vienna before they arrived in town and wait for them at the train station. I told the people at my hotel that I was looking for these two Italian girls. They looked at me like I was nuts and told me that there are 1.2 million people in the city. My simple little task was turning into quite a daunting project.

I put myself in their shoes—what would they do first when they got into town? I went to the train station and asked the information booth for the names of some cheap hostels nearby. They gave me a pretty long list. Then I got the schedule of all the trains they could conceivably be on from Munich. It turns out that Vienna is the *crossroads* of that part of Europe, and there were trains from Munich every hour or so. When I went to the hostel nearest to the train station, they weren't there, so I decided to leave a note on the bulletin board. Then I returned to the station and waited for the next train. When they didn't arrive, I moved on to the next youth hostel on the list. This was my routine for three whole days. I returned every night to my hotel exhausted. The people at the hotel thought it was kind of funny, but they were cheering me on. At the same time, they knew it was an impossible and nutty idea.

Finally, at one hostel, the woman at the front desk told me Alessandra was there. I had found her! I went up to her room and I could hear two female voices inside, but they wouldn't open the door! I was heartbroken. Maybe she didn't want to see me, after all. I hadn't slept for a week and paranoia was getting the best of me.

My quest was over. I had tried and failed. I'd done everything I could, and I still couldn't find her. I was convinced I had done such a thorough job—Alessandra was either not in Vienna or she didn't want to see me. That was the end of the story. I guessed it was the end of our romance, too.

The next morning in my hotel, I got a call from the front desk saying someone was there to see me. Alessandra! It wasn't her behind that hostel door I was pounding on, after all. It turned out that on their way to Vienna out they had taken a detour to Bavaria to see some castles. When they arrived in Vienna, they did exactly what I predicted—got a list of hostels and went to the one closest to the station. Alessandra happened to wander over to the bulletin board, and she saw my note to her. She wasn't even looking for a message and didn't expect me to be in town.

So many circumstances tried to obstruct our reunion, but it happened, anyway. We must have been drawn together by some mysterious forces.

In Vienna, our romance really blossomed. It was a complete fairy tale. I was thirty-one years old, she was twenty-one. Having seen a little more of the world, I had learned that seemingly impossible things could happen and actually end up making sense. I didn't worry about what would come next between Alessandra and me. I was just enjoying the here and now. She was holding back a little because she didn't see any future for us. But you never know what's going to happen.

Our parting in Rome was a sad one. It was the end of the summer, and I returned home to California. We began writing and calling each other and we decided that I would visit her at Christmas. Still, I wasn't letting myself get serious about her, because nothing about this pairing made any sense. My mind, however, remained open. I looked at this string of coincidences and improbable events that led to our meeting. There must have been a reason behind all of that. I even started studying Italian. It wouldn't hurt for me to make a little effort!

When the holidays rolled around, however, I asked myself why I was doing this. I hadn't seen her in months, and I began to have serious doubts about the whole thing. By then my crush on Alessandra had disappeared. I rationalized that maybe that was because we hadn't seen each other in so long. The only reason I went to Italy at all was that I *remembered* having a crush on her. Worst-case scenario: I could always leave Alessandra earlier than planned and see some more of Europe.

It was over Christmas that we fell in love with each other. Once I saw her again, all the reasons I followed her around that castle came rushing back to me. Alessandra captivated me. She was always really happy and upbeat and bouncy. She was just fun. I was in love with a girl who lived in Italy—with her parents, no less!

I did anything I could do to make this relationship happen. I did the financial analysis—this is where having an engineering background comes in. The only thing to do, I decided, was to move back into my parents' house so I could afford the thirty trips to Italy that I took over the next few years. That alone should prove how much I loved her!

During our long-distance relationship, it never occurred to me that I would lose her or we'd break up. I thought we'd figure out how to make everything work. I never worried because I knew in my heart she and I belonged to each other. We got married twice, once in the United States and once in the Amalfi coast, and Alessandra joined me in California, where we're now raising our family.

It was a noble adventure we both embarked on that day in Salzburg. The funny thing is that I never would have chased her around the castle had she not smiled at me on the *fonicolare*. Years later she told me I was wrong about that—she never even saw me.

Norm and Ellen

accountant, 61; lawyer, 56
married March 9, 1986

♥

My family and friends had all given up on me. I was forty-seven years old and had never even been *close* to marriage. Everyone thought I was destined to spend my life by myself.

I, however, never lost hope. I tried all sorts of things to meet women, and I went on lots of dates. Usually, there would be no second date because I could tell right away if it wasn't going to work. I thought of myself as an example of the law of averages. Some people get married at eighteen and some at forty-seven. I just happened to be one of the later ones. But I always held on to the idea that someday I might meet a woman I wanted to marry.

One weekend, I went to my cousin's wedding in Pittsburgh, and a female rabbi from New York was seated at the same table I was. I don't know what made her ask about the status of my social life. Perhaps she could just tell it could use a little jump start. I told her my personal life was pretty terrible. And she offered to set me up. By this time I had said to myself a million times, *No more blind dates!* But the matchmaker, after all, was a rabbi. This was almost an edict handed down from heaven. The rabbi had no one particular in mind for me, but she took my card and promised to call.

The rabbi knew Ellen from the synagogue, and one day as she was giving Ellen a ride home, it dawned on her that Ellen was the one for me. The rabbi likes to boast that as soon as the idea hit her, she knew right then and there the match was going to take.

I met Ellen for the first time in December, when we went out for Sunday brunch. It was a bright, cold sunny day, and we took a walk in Central Park and read the Sunday *Times*. She was very attractive, and I knew right away that I wanted to see her again. Coming from me, the one-date wonder, this was big! The very next day, I called to make plans with her for the holidays and New Year's Eve. We spent a lot of time celebrating with all of our family and friends. It was so easy and comfortable to be around Ellen. My family loved her, and already it felt like she belonged in my life. It was the right fit.

One night we were out with another couple and as the two women were engrossed in a conversation, we men had a heated debate about pro basketball. I knew there was one Jewish man in the NBA Hall of Fame, but I couldn't remember his name. Ellen overheard this and even though she was in the middle of her own conversation, she turned to me and simply said, "Dolph Schayes," and continued talking to her friend without missing a beat. That's the moment I fell in love with her.

After the winter holidays, I realized I had yet to thank the rabbi for the introduction. I called her up and told her about how excited I was about meeting Ellen. The rabbi's exact words to me were, "Well, what are you waiting for?" "Waiting for?" I said. "It's only been two weeks!" "Well," she countered, "It didn't take my husband that long." After I hung up her words kept echoing in my head. I knew that I loved Ellen, and suddenly it dawned on me that if I waited too long, I might lose her. I thought, *I'm forty-seven years old, and I'm not going to blow this one.* . . .

My mother had died many years earlier, and since all of my siblings were already married, they saved her diamond wedding ring for me to give to my future wife. My sister, who had met Ellen over the holidays, called to ask about how things were going, and she reminded me that I had mother's ring. When I told my sister that I had already taken it out of the safety-deposit box, she started crying! No one expected that poor diamond would be gathering dust for sixteen years, waiting for me to find a wife. There is absolutely no way to describe how happy my friends and family were.

I proposed to Ellen on Valentine's Day, just two months after we met. We were in one of the most romantic places in New York, the Oak Room at the Algonquin Hotel, when I gave her a little box wrapped in the theater section of the paper. She unwrapped it very slowly, refusing to look at me. When she opened the box, the tears started rolling down her face, and she didn't say a word. I asked her, "Ellen, do you like it?" She nodded and then I said, "Well, if you want to keep it, you have to marry me." Finally she nodded again. She agreed to be my wife.

At our wedding, the rabbi was almost more emotional than Ellen and I were. We tried to have a small gathering in Ellen's mother's apartment, but people were so excited they told us they were showing up whether we wanted them to or not. We ended up with about sixty wedding crashers, and it was the most wonderful ceremony in the world.

Often, I stop and think about how truly fortunate I am. It was just sheer luck that the rabbi came to my cousin's wedding and was seated near me. I waited such a long time to get married. And now I know the reason: I was waiting for Ellen. We were just passing the time until we found each other. The really good news is that fourteen years later, our marriage just keeps getting better and better.

Karen and Don

meeting planner, 29; securities trader, 29

married August 16, 1997

♥

The dreaded letter arrived in the mail. "The City of New York requires you, under penalty of the law, to report for civil jury duty on Monday, at 8:00 A.M." Ugh! What could be worse? At least with criminal jury duty, there might be a little excitement or drama. But nothing could be duller than civil cases. There was no getting out of it. I was doomed to two weeks of utter boredom.

I spent the entire first week in that jury room waiting to be called on a case. Everyone was checking each other out. And the men were beyond awful. The entire experience was hideous. I just couldn't wait for it all to be over. In the meantime, I had read just about all of *Crime and Punishment*. I thought that was an appropriate book for the occasion.

The next Monday, I arrived resigned to another mind-numbing week. But as I sat down in the jury room, I happened to notice a man who looked a bit familiar. I thought he might have gone to my college, Johns Hopkins, although we had never met. During roll when they called out his name, I realized it *was* him. He was totally adorable and cute. He had really short hair and was very preppy. That day, Don was wearing a Polo shirt and great-fitting Levis. I did happen to notice—quite by accident—that he had a great body. There was just one thing: he wore these terrible, chunky Coke-bottle glasses. They reminded me of a poor six-year-old's first pair of glasses. It was sad.

After lunch, I decided to strategically place myself in the jury room near him. I sat a row or two behind him, so that if he turned around to look at the clock, I'd be right in his line of vision. It was a brilliant plan. Sure enough, he turned around and saw me. He recognized me, but I played it cool. "Don't I know you from somewhere?" he asked. Pretending to see him for the first time, I said, "Oh, yes, sure." We talked about school and people we knew and the books we were reading. He had just finished a biography on Truman and offered to lend it to me.

Now, you can't doll yourself up too much for jury duty, or it's pretty obvious. The next day, I wanted to look nice, so I upgraded my usual jeans to a little skirt and a cute shirt. When I walked into the jury room, Don was on the phone. We waved and acknowledged each other. Whatever he was doing sounded pretty important. He was yelling into the receiver, "Buy! Sell! Do this! Do that! Call me! Gotta go!" I was duly impressed. Much later, he confessed that he planned to be on the phone pretending to be wheeling and dealing so I would overhear him when I came in. The whole thing was a sham.

We sat down together to wait out the hours. For our lunch break, Don and I agreed eat together at a great place nearby. Now, I'm completely obsessed with food and was very curious to see what he was going to order. We both chose the same thing: grilled tuna steak sandwich. I was thinking giddily, *He likes grilled tuna, I love grilled tuna! Excellent.* Then the conversation moved on to cereal, and he mentioned how much he loved it. Me, too! I was thinking, *He loves cereal. We both loved cereal!* He matched my food obsession bite by bite as we started talking about how a cereal can't be composed of just flakes. The flakes need to be balanced by a crunch to prevent a soggy situation. We were eye to eye on this very important issue. But then, I discovered something terrible about Don. He loved whole milk. I drank only skim and thought anything else was revolting. Maybe this relationship wasn't going to work after all! Even still, we had a great lunch together. He was so funny and perfect. After I paid for lunch, he said it would only be right if I'd let him take me to dinner. *Yes!*

He wanted to go out that very same night, but I didn't want to look like I had no life, so I told him I had plans and we met the next evening. It was a really warm April night, so we went for a long walk after dinner. As we were strolling, we had the best conversation. I was excitedly thinking to myself, *We are really hitting it off. Things are going great here.* Later, Don shared with me his recollection of the night: we went to dinner, took a walk, and I wouldn't shut up! He was wondering, *How can I get this girl to stop talking?* We've had a good laugh over that. Back at Don's apartment, I was checking out one of his books when he leaned over and just kissed me. It was magical. After I got home, I called an old childhood friend and told her I was going to marry Don.

We started dating immediately, and it was wonderful. To my relief I learned that Don usually wore contacts instead of those awful glasses. Much later, when we moved in together, the glasses got lost during our move. To this day, Don believes that I threw them out. But I really didn't. With or without glasses, though, Don is adorable.

Our relationship has had its ups and downs, with a few break-ups and reconciliations. But eventually, we realized we couldn't live without each other. When Don told me he loved me and wanted to marry me, I knew he meant it with all his heart. We joke now that we should do a public service announcement promoting jury duty. It wasn't so bad, after all.

Paul and Mimi

film industry analyst, 38; salesperson, 26

married August 21, 1999

♥

$\mathcal{I}$t was September 5, 1997, and I had to go to the Los Angeles airport really early in the morning to fly to Seattle for my nephew's wedding. Once I checked in at the gate, I sat down in terminal one to wait for flight 98 to be called. Right away I noticed this gorgeous young lady leaning against the wall, talking to her friend. The minute I looked at her, our eyes met. I caught her staring at me, too. We exchanged quick glances and smiled at each other. I thought, *Oh wow, she's really beautiful. I have been single too long!*

I knew I was going to marry her the minute I saw her. She was the one. I was totally hooked. I've never felt that way about anybody before. It was a just metaphysical feeling.

The airline started loading the plane, and she was on my flight. On this airline, there were no seat reservations, it's just a cattle call. So I thought, *I've got to sit next to her.* I came up with a plan:

I was going to get on the plane after she did, so I could plop myself down in the seat right next to her. But there was a problem: all the passengers had cards with numbers on them, and the people with the lowest numbers were supposed to board first. As she and I walked up to the gate at the same time, the flight attendant told me, "Oh, no sir, you go first." I had a lower number than she did. My plan was foiled!

After I sat down, I saw her get on and thought, *Please, please, please sit somewhere near me.* And even though there was a seat open right next to me, she sat in the row right in front of me instead. I leaned over and delivered my big pickup line: "I'm really sorry I cut in front of you, but the flight attendant made me do it." She smiled and told me not to worry about it. I eavesdropped on her conversation with the elderly couple next to her, and she was so nice and friendly, treating them like they were her grandparents. I thought she was a really genuine person.

The flight had a stopover in Oakland, and when we stood up to stretch our legs, somehow she and I started talking again. We talked the whole way up to Seattle. She was still in the row in front of me but she turned around in her seat to face me the whole time. I told her about how I went to Hawaii by myself because I couldn't find anyone to go with me, playing up the pathetic bachelor thing. She told me about how she hated L.A. and couldn't wait to get back home. *Oh, great,* I thought, *a strike against me.* Already I was wondering if this was going to be a problem because I wanted to leave open the possibility that she'd come back to southern California.

Nobody can explain love, but we had chemistry. I just fell in love with her right on the spot. Mimi was the perfect person for me. She was sensitive and she cared about other people's thoughts and feelings. I just felt an immediate tie, a bond. I was totally taken with her and. Finally, there came the big moment of truth: we got to Seattle and had to go our separate ways. It was funny because before I could even say anything, she gave me her phone number. Cool! One of her girlfriends came to pick her up, and we hugged good-bye. No kissing, of course. After she walked away I couldn't stop thinking about her. At my nephew's wedding that weekend, I told all my relatives that I had just met the most beautiful woman.

Now, I'd seen the movie *Swingers* so I knew the rule: you wait five days before calling a woman. I had scared someone off before because I had called her too soon. I'd learned my lesson, and I wasn't going to blow it this time, even though I desperately wanted to call Mimi right away. I was dying! I waited until after I was back home.

When I phoned her the first time, she told me she had been wondering when the hell I was going to call! She had expected her phone to ring that very first weekend. We talked that night for five hours straight, and she invited me to visit her in Seattle.

Right away we established that we were crazy about each other. I began going back and forth to Seattle and racking up the frequent flyer miles. She came to visit me, too. We were having so much fun that she didn't even mind L.A. too much. I knew I couldn't let this girl get away. We couldn't commute forever and she wasn't going to move to my city just to be my girlfriend. She had sort of put out some vibes that she might be open to the idea of getting married.

The day after Christmas that year, Mimi was flying to L.A. to see me. Without her knowing it, I snuck up to Seattle so that I could join her as a surprise on her flight to see me. The next morning the fog rolled in, and our flight was delayed for *hours*. Mimi started calling my apartment in L.A. and leaving messages saying, "Paul, where are you!?" She didn't know at that exact moment I was watching her run to the phone booth every few minutes to call me and tell me she might be changing planes or switching airlines. I called in to get my messages about fifty times. And with each message, she was getting more upset saying, "Where the hell are you?!" I was sweating bullets. My big plan was going up in smoke and I was freaking out. I was literally hiding and ducking behind things in the terminal so she wouldn't see me.

Then there was an announcement: our flight was finally boarding. I snuck onto the plane after everyone had taken their seats. The flight attendant got on the speaker and announced: "Mimi, please come to the front of the airplane." I saw her stomping down the aisle, and I was shaking from nervousness. She came up to the flight attendant and snapped, "What!?" She had already had the *worst* day. The attendant said, "Ma'am, you're in trouble. You're going to have to turn around." When she spun around, I was standing there with the bottle of champagne. She burst into tears before I could even say anything. I got down on one knee and told her that even though it had only been a few months since we first met, I knew the moment I laid eyes on her that I wanted to spend the rest of my life with her. And I gave her a beautiful square-cut diamond ring that was made just for her.

She said yes and kept on crying. They announced our big news to the entire plane and everyone applauded while we walked back to our seats and shared champagne toasts with the passengers around us.

It's a cliché, but I always knew there was somebody out there in the world who was just for me. And I'm so lucky, because I actually found that person. I think the most interesting thing is, what were the chances that I would meet Mimi? I almost didn't go to that wedding. I didn't want to get up so early to take that flight. And Mimi hadn't planned on being in L.A. that weekend. There were so many what-ifs. It wasn't like we worked in the same place every day and had two years to run into each other. We had one moment in time to find each other, and we did. It was meant to be.

Ilissa and David

human resources executive, 32; computer consultant, 33

married August 20, 1994

♥

It was hate at first sight. I met David at the end of my first year in law school, the night before my very first final. My first law school exam ever. So I was completely frazzled and stressed. My friend Joe insisted I take a break from my frantic studying to have dinner with him and a few friends. I showed up looking like hell and feeling like hell.

I looked at Joe's two friends, Jeff and David, and I thought David was the biggest dork I'd ever seen. I didn't pay any attention to him. He was skinny, bald, and funny-looking—no question about it. And he was the *worst* dresser.

We went to a seedy Italian place called Ralph's, where the big thing to do is to order a group salad that arrives in one big bowl. David served up the salad meticulously, like this: *Olive, olive, olive, olive. Tomato, tomato, tomato, tomato,* doling out one to each of us. Meanwhile, I was neurotically rushed and getting madder and madder thinking, *What is this guy doing?!* Finally, I yanked the salad bowl away from him and snapped, "I'll serve it myself!" He, of course, thought I was the biggest bitch. To this day, nine years later, he will never serve salad in my presence.

A year passed, and I had a part in a law school performance, and David happened to be directing the show. Somewhere in the midst of all the rehearsals, I suddenly noticed he was really funny and much cuter than I originally thought. He wasn't a dork, after all. I guess he decided I was cute, too. So we became friends and confidants. Meanwhile, I was dating a hunky blond football player and was debating whether or not to marry him. I asked David for his advice and he told me boldly, "Break up with him and sleep with me." David was relentless. He just put it all on the table.

It was April when David announced, "I have a prediction: You're going to have sex with me on May eleventh." Instead of being completely offended, I just said, "Yeah, yeah, whatever." I was starting to warm up to him. He was very persuasive, and definitely persistent.

After our last final exams, we decided to go out to a movie, and I reminded him we were just going as friends. But David lived right in the theater district, and he suggested we try to get last-minute tickets to a Broadway show instead.

We were in front of *I Hate Hamlet* when a limo pulled up and out jumped Joan Rivers. So David walked right up to her and said, "Hey, Joan, got two tickets for me?" When he told her his price range, she said, "Good luck!" and the whole crowd around us laughed. We got into the show and at intermission saw Joan Rivers again. She teased David, saying, "Who let you in here?" He teased her right back. I loved the way he was outspoken and extremely charismatic.

After the show we went to a retro diner with goofy music,

strippers, and strolling tattoo artists. While we were waiting for a table, in walked Joan. David gave her a hard time about following us and told the maître d', "Joan's a friend of mine, give her a good table." We ended up sitting next to her for dinner, and to our surprise, Joan even picked up our tab.

It was the best, most hilarious night of my life. I was shocked, mortified, and laughing all at once. One thing about my husband, he's a lot of fun, and that's why I married him.

I went home with David that night and never left him again. The football player was history. It was May third! A full week ahead of his deadline.

Jodi and Aaron

high school teacher, 29; software engineer, 32

married June 20, 1998

♥

$\mathcal{I}$ met my husband through a keyboard and a computer screen. We both worked for America Online, and a coworker of mine had corresponded with Aaron in a chat room. Knowing Aaron was single, she introduced us electronically. We flirted for a bit, and it was all innocent enough. A few nights later, I logged on and chatted with him again, and he mentioned how tired his eyes were from spending so much time on the computer. I seized the opportunity and hinted to him subtly, "You know, you could call me." My phone rang a moment later, and we talked for seven and a half hours that night. During that marathon conversation, I learned that he was witty, kind, hugely sensitive, and caring about other people. I got a strange feeling in my stomach whenever I thought about him. The next night we talked six hours on the telephone. Even though we had never met and it was *really* fast, we decided we were boyfriend and girlfriend.

Jeez, did I feel like I was about twelve years old. I was giddy, and we wanted to share our happiness with our on-line friends. With Valentine's Day coming up, we thought it would be fun to have an on-line wedding, otherwise known as a "weeding" among the chat-room crowd. "Weedings" have been happening on the Internet for a while, and is comparable to getting "pinned" in the old days. It wasn't a joke at all. Aaron and I wanted to make a commitment to each other. So we started preparing for our pseudowedding, and it became a big to-do, with pretend invitations, attendants, musicians—you name it.

The next night, another on-line friend, Doreen, told me about a brunch that our AOL coworkers in San Francisco were planning for a few days later. Aaron happened to live there while I lived in Chicago, and I joked about how funny if would be if I just showed up, surprising my soon-to-be "weeded husband." Even though we were kidding around, the wheels in my mind were already spinning. The next day, I booked my flight to the Bay Area. Doreen concocted some story to get Aaron to come over to her place in San Francisco so that he would be there when I arrived.

On the flight, I was so nervous I could barely breathe. As I walked into Doreen's apartment, she said to Aaron casually, "Hey . . . look who I found." My first thought was, *Thank God . . . he IS cute!* Second thought: *Why is he just staring at me like that? He's repulsed by me!* He knew exactly who I was because he had seen my picture. Aaron was just in pure and utter shock, especially since he had just spoken to me in Chicago on the phone a few hours earlier. Then tears formed in both of our eyes, and we held hands and touched each other's faces—for the next eight hours. That first day, we both confessed our love for each other and began talking about my moving to California.

The day after we met was our on-line weeding. Instead of it being a cross-country virtual ceremony, Aaron sat in his office on his desktop computer, and I was just a few feet away, using his laptop. The next day, we checked into a local hotel for our honeymoon. He brought a box of pictures of his family and friends and pointed out who was who in each photo. When we finished, he took my hands, looked into my eyes, and asked if I would marry him. There were tears. Many, many tears! Then a gulp, a nod, and a "YES!" This was just two days after we met for the first time. I'd be lying if I said I wasn't nervous about getting engaged so quickly. But it was never the kind of nervousness that makes you really wonder if it's right. I had known from the moment I laid eyes on him that it was. To paraphrase *When Harry Met Sally* . . . : "We just knew. We knew the way you know about a good melon."

Fran and Steve

lawyer, 36; financier, 52
married October 4, 1997

♥

$\mathcal{I}$t was because of a blizzard and a snowbank that I happened to meet my husband. My friend Rachel and I went up to Killington, Vermont, for a ski weekend. After the first day on the slopes—and a brief stop for happy hour—we tried to drive back to our ski house, but the snow was coming down intensely. The visibility on the roads was zero. We decided to just abandon the car in a parking lot, walk back up to the ski resort village, and hunker down at one of the nearby hotels for the night.

When we returned to the bar, everyone was in the snowstorm spirit. The windows were covered from the blizzard, and the cars were completely buried outside. Rachel happened to notice a guy sitting at the bar wearing a baseball cap who she thought was kind of cute. I helped her out by starting up a conversation with this guy, Chris. What are friends for? Chris introduced us to his friend, Steve. He was wearing black sweats, a T-shirt, and a fanny pack. I was not interested in him at all. I had *no* conscious thought about Steve.

A little later, Rachel and I decided we were ready to leave, and Steve offered to give us a ride, even though the inn where we were staying was about ten steps away. He *insisted.* This meant he had to dig his car out from underneath mounds of snow. But as he was driving, he made an unfortunate wrong turn. This was a crucial event: Steve decided to make a U-turn and in the process got stuck in a snowbank. So now he was blocking all these cars along with someone's driveway. There was nothing we could do. By this time it was late and I was just sick of the whole thing. Chris and Steve were stuck on the mountain with us and had nowhere to sleep. So I said, "I'm really tired, I'm leaving but you're welcome to stay with us if you want." And I just got out of the car and walked to the inn while they followed behind.

We let the guys stay in our room, but Rachel and I shared one big bed while they were in another one. There was no way any funny business was happening between us and these guys. I was going to sleep—that was it. Steve wasn't picking up my signals, though. He kept on talking to me, even after we were all in bed and the lights were out. Eventually, Rachel broke the news to him that I had fallen asleep.

The next morning I woke up and the first thing I heard was this wonderful voice saying, "This is Steve in room P3 and I want to cancel my wake-up call." My very first thought was—and this is *really* weird—*This is the man I'm going to marry.* And I wasn't even attracted to him. He did have a great, sexy voice. He sounded like he belonged on a radio talk show. Later that morning I was complaining of a headache, and Steve magically appeared with coffee and aspirin. Everything started to change.

Chris and Steve hung out with us for the rest of the afternoon and brought dinner back to our place that night. I had a feeling Rachel might like Steve, and if she did, being a loyal friend I wasn't going to pursue him. But Rachel made it clear she had no interest in Steve. When they arrived for dinner, dressed up in their nice khakis, Rachel and I were both pretty nervous! I hung back a little but then I heard Steve asking, "Where's Fran? Where's Fran?" I thought that was a good sign. And then at the table during dinner, I was happy when Steve held my hand.

A few months later, I found out that the night that Steve and Chris were stranded with us at the inn, they actually had plans to stay with friends whose house was right across the street from where Steve's car got stuck. We got conned. Steve told me he conveniently forgot to mention that because he wanted to be with me. It's a good thing he was so persistent or we never would have gotten together. There were obstacles along the way, I'm not going to deny that. For one thing, there's the age gap. He's also been married before and has three sons. So there were things I had to think about. But I have a great time with Steve, and I know he's the one for me. I love his personality, his serenity, and his calming presence in my life.

Tim and Cora

police officer, 36; physician's assistant, 31

married August 30, 1997

♥

$\mathcal{T}$he first time I met my wife, I didn't buy her a drink or give her flowers: I wrote her a speeding ticket. I was working as a state trooper in Kingston, New York. One summer, I happened to stop a vehicle speeding on Route 209, and issued the operator a ticket. The speed limit was 55 mph, but this woman was doing 70 or 72, easy. When I pulled her over, she was very friendly and courteous to try to sweet-talk me out of the ticket, but I wrote her up anyway. I wasn't even thinking about whether she was cute or not.

About a month later, I received a trial notice in the mail. The driver, Cora, was trying to get the fine reduced, so a date was set and we all went to court. It turned out that Cora was friends with another trooper at my station. He vouched for her good character, and since she had a clean driving record, we all agreed to let her off with a seventy-five-dollar fine, and no points on her license.

That day in the courthouse, while the lawyers and Cora and I were all conferring in the hallways, I noticed for the first time how attractive she was. But as a trooper, I stop a lot of people. Some of them are good looking, some of them aren't. I never think too much about it. I had no idea that anything was going to ever come of my chance encounter with this woman.

A few months later, at Christmastime, I was hanging out with a few friends at a restaurant in Albany, where I had since been transferred for work. We were sitting at the bar, eating and having a few drinks, when I noticed that the bartender looked familiar. Then I figured out how I knew her: she was the speeding lady from Route 209.

She didn't recognize me at all, so I didn't remind her about the ticket incident, for a while at least. Then toward the end of the evening, I told my friends I had to work early in the morning and that I had to get going. Overhearing this, Cora decided to bust my chops and said to me, "I didn't think McDonald's opened that early." I took the opening and asked her if she recognized me. When she admitted she didn't, I reminded her, "We met this summer in Kingston on Route 209, speedy." All of a sudden her face turned bright red. She was so embarrassed. But after she regained her composure, she thought it was funny, and we yukked it up a little.

I knew that night that we were both interested in each other. Definitely. I got a chance to see her real personality for the first time. She was very strong willed and she didn't take flak from anyone—even me. But at the time, she had a boyfriend and I had a girlfriend. After the night at the bar, neither one of us pursued each other.

It was an odd coincidence that she and I ran into each other in Albany, fifty miles from the site of the ticket. As it turned out,

Cora was living and working in Albany, and I had recently moved there. The day I pulled her over, she just happened to be driving past my squad car while going to visit her parents in Kingston. This is where fate came in. Over the next three or four years, I ran into Cora around town several times. I'd be out with friends and I'd see her with her sister or boyfriend. We'd say hello and make small talk. There was definitely an interest there, but the timing was just never right.

The third time I ran into her, she was with her boyfriend. After I said good-bye to her, I talked to my sister about the situation and told her how much I liked this girl who was always unavailable. I could really see myself getting involved with her, I confessed. But still, Cora was taken.

A while later, I broke up with the girl I had been seeing and started thinking about Cora again. I was curious about what she was doing. I didn't even know her number, so I looked her up in the phone book. But when I called, it was her sister who answered the phone. After waiting all this time to make my move, Cora had moved away. She now lived on Long Island, about four hours from Albany.

I mustered up the nerve to call her up and ask her out on a date, anyway. On the phone she delivered some good news. She had broken up with her boyfriend. Finally! Cora was planning on coming up to Albany to visit her sister, so we decided to go out while she was in town. Little did I know, Cora planned on bringing her sister along on our first date. She was kind of like our chaperone. I actually didn't mind that her sister joined us. The three of us went out to a few bars and met up with some mutual friends. It was all very casual and easy. But it was obvious that Cora and I were hitting it off. We were just taking slow, small steps and seeing how things worked. At this point, I had already waited four years for Cora and I was willing to be a little more patient. Our timing was finally right.

We had seen each other a few times when Cora asked me to come visit her on Long Island for the first time. We spent a romantic day on the beach and by the pool in her backyard. That night, I made a big pronouncement: I told her that I knew we were going to get married someday. She just looked at me and said, "Is this a line?" But it really wasn't. I just had a good feeling about us. This was it. After all, I didn't drive four hours for just anybody.

Cora and I dated long distance for a year and had a great time every time we saw each other. We always had so much fun when we were together. I learned that she is a very hardworking person and is very independent. Cora also has a great sense of humor. And, even more important, she tolerated my poor sense of humor. A few months into the relationship, we were walking on the beach one day and I said to her, "Wouldn't this be a romantic place to get engaged?" She warned me then, "You'd better be a little more creative than that." I wasn't even planning anything that day, but after that, the pressure was on. Should there come a time when I was ready to ask her to marry me, I knew I had to come up with a pretty impressive proposal.

A few months later, Cora came up to Albany for Father's Day. I told her I had to go to work that morning at seven, and she was going to spend the day at a family party in Kingston. Instead of going to work after I left home, though, I turned my car toward Kingston and drove to Cora's parents' house.

I told them I wanted to marry their daughter and asked them for their permission. They were so touched and excited about it. I let them in on how I had decided to propose, and they thought it was such a great idea, they ran to borrow a neighbor's video camera and made me promise to tape it. Cora hadn't arrived yet, so they called her to find out exactly what time she was leaving Albany and when they could expect her.

My next stop was to pick up a fellow trooper who was going to help me with my plan. He and I drove a squad car to the thruway exit where I knew Cora would be getting off on her way to see her parents. We were lying in wait to the side of the toll plaza. I was feeling very relaxed and was having fun with the whole thing. I even had the videocamera out and was narrating the day's events so far. I said, "It's June 16, 1996, and our target today is Cora Lynn, who's a predicate violator of a vehicle in traffic law." But as soon as I saw Cora drive through the toll plaza, my heart started pounding. I told my friend, "We're not video-taping anything!" And that was the end of the camera.

As Cora passed us, we pulled out and followed her for a mile or two. Once we got to Route 209, my buddy and I flashed our lights and pulled her over in the exact same place where I stopped her five years earlier, almost to the day. The other trooper got out of the car, walked up to Cora, and told her we had a report of a white Acura speeding on the thruway. I knew she wouldn't be able to argue that one; she's got a lead foot. (Even I haven't been able to change that.) The trooper asked her for her license and registration.

While she was still fumbling around looking for her paperwork, I sneaked up to the side of her car and said, "Excuse me, I've been looking for you." She looked up at me in shock and asked what I was doing there. "Well," I said, "I've got something I want to say to you." With that, I opened her car door, got down on one knee and recited a speech I prepared ahead of time: "Our paths crossed here on this road five years ago. Since then, I'm very fortunate that our paths happened to cross a few more times.

- 55 -

I want you to know that I love you very much and I want our paths to be one and the same from this day forward. Will you marry me?" And her response: "I thought you'd never ask!"

She told me later she didn't hear a word I'd said. She was too worried some tractor trailer would come by and run into me kneeling there on the side of the road. But since then, she'd heard me retell this story a thousand times.

Cora and I married a year later and now we have a little running cop joke between us: "She paid the fine, I'm doing the time!"

Gina and Bob

children's theater director and guidance counselor, 51;
small business owner, 54
married February 1, 1969

♥

One of my friends set Bob and me up on a blind date. She just said, "There's a great guy I really want you to meet. Double-date with us." We decided to go to a Sergio Mendez concert.

At the time I was a junior in college, majoring in dance at San Diego State. And I was pretty liberal, picketing to throw R.O.T.C. off campus. I was very serious about the protesting and very vocal about my political feelings. I thought the war in Vietnam was just so wrong. Writing letters and going to rallies could have been my full-time occupation if my life hadn't been tempered by dancing.

The night before we were all to go out, my blind date, Bob, and his buddy dropped by my apartment to hang out with my friend and me. The first time I saw him and he looked at me, I thought, *I have to remember this moment so I can tell our children how I met their father.* Then I thought, *You're sick, Gina, you're really sick!* But this message just came into my head and everything crystallized. It was like I could see my whole future unfolding. It was bad enough I knew I was going to marry this person, I was already mapping out our family. It was so out of character for me. Once he left, I told my roommate Suzie about my premonition. And I found out later that when Bob walked out of my apartment, he turned to his friend and said, "That's the girl I'm going to marry."

It wasn't until the night that we first went out that I learned the horrible truth: Bob was in R.O.T.C. He told me, and quite surprisingly, I did not flip out. He had a very logical explanation: He was in his fourth year in school and very close to getting drafted. He didn't want to go to Vietnam and get shot. Rather than being a "ground pounder," as he used to say, Bob thought he'd have more control over his life as an officer. Nobody, absolutely *nobody*, wanted to be drafted into the army. In the army, there was a very realistic fear you would die. I gained respect for his decision.

With Bob, it wasn't like lust at first sight, it was more like comfortable love at first sight. And he was so very different than the guys I normally went out with. He was more like my really good friend. Being with him was just right. I knew we would be together.

Two weeks into this relationship, my eccentric roommate and I decided to put a spell on Bob to see if we could get him to propose. What can I say—we were in college and crazy. We actually read a book of spells that called for a bunch of strange ingredients and the blood of a lamb, so we got some lamb chops and tried to squeeze the juice out. We did the best we could, and we laughed and laughed. I think we gave Bob something to eat with this concoction in it. The scary part was, that night Bob *did* ask me to marry him! I was shocked. The spell had clearly worked. We'd only gone out for two weeks, but I already knew that I loved him and I said yes. Bob was very sweet and sympathetic and understanding.

The very next day we went to a wedding and I caught the bouquet and he caught the garter belt. That's when I started to believe we were really going to get married. I jumped up and yelled, "Whooo! It's true, it's true!" Bob turned absolutely white. I'd been pinned before, but this was real. It was just going to happen this way.

We were married in the middle of the school year four months later. Poor Bob, he never even really had a serious girlfriend before me. And this happened so fast. It was crazy. *Crazy.* In the middle of my last senior-year finals, I was having labor pains with my first child. To this day, thirty-one years later, Bob blames my spell and claims that garter belt landed on him accidentally.

For years, every once in a while, Bob would tell me how many weeks and hours it had been since we were first introduced. We used to celebrate those Thursdays—the day we met.

Steve and Nancy

lawyer, 34; lawyer, 30
married September 30, 1995

♥

*T*he first time I laid eyes on Nancy, I fell in love with her. This is true. I thought she was so beautiful. Immediately, I knew I had to ask her out. It was the last day of my internship at the law department for the city of New York and the first day of hers. Our paths just barely crossed.

That day I brought into the office a coffee cake that my grandmother had baked. Nancy later told me I got big points for that. Why, I'm not really sure. Somehow, she concluded I was a really nice guy. The thought never once entered my mind that somehow my grandmother's coffee cake was going to help get me a woman!

Later that week there was a law school party at a local bar, and I knew Nancy would be there with her friends. It was a twenty-dollar all-you-can-drink night. So I, of course, went right at eight to get the most for my money. I was kind of seeing someone at the time and she was there, too, hanging all over me.

I was trying to get rid of her before Nancy showed up. She was nice and cute but there was nothing really there. By the time Nancy arrived, I was pretty drunk and didn't make the greatest impression on her.

Nancy didn't even want to talk to me. Finally, I asked her to dance and got her phone number too. This being a Thursday, I didn't call her until Sunday. I already had plans for the weekend and assumed she did, too. When I finally called, she almost didn't go out with me because I had waited three days.

Luckily, she acted against the advice of her friends and came to dinner with me. That first night she talked the whole time. She barely touched her meal. So I ended up eating my dinner *and* hers. I never had that problem of talking and eating simultaneously. It turned out that Nancy and I both went to the same law school but we never met. She also claims that she went to the same bar I hung out at every Thursday night. But I never saw her and she never saw me. And I would have remembered her. Later that evening, I came on a little too strong, which was strange because I'm never like that. I mean, I didn't attack her or anything. But once more, I almost blew it with her entirely. In retrospect, things could easily have ended with that date.

But she did go out with me again, and six months later I knew I wanted to marry her. Nancy is such a caring and understanding person. I feel good just being around her. She's also very funny and can be stubborn, but in the long run it's a good thing because she doesn't let me get away with much. It was a few years until I actually proposed to her. For her law school graduation present, I took her to a bed and breakfast in Connecticut for the weekend. I arranged for roses to be in the room when we got there, and that night at dinner, I popped the question. After the main course the waiter brought out dessert menus that I had specially made and sent to the inn ahead of time. One of the desserts was called "Sweet Engagement" and the description read, "This dessert will last an entire lifetime full of love and happiness. The person sitting next to you would love to spend the rest of his life with you."

Nancy thought it was something chocolate and tried to order it. Once I pulled out the ring, though, she figured it out.

At the wedding, we thanked my grandmother for her coffee cake, which made everything else possible.

Irene and Steve

technical support specialist, 45; graphic artist, 39

married July 4, 1997

♥

I had been single for a couple of years, *really* single. I had been in a series of difficult relationships and had realized that I had no understanding of who I was and what I wanted. With one boyfriend, I literally consulted him on every grocery item on my shopping list. "Quilted paper towels or regular?" I was not capable of making decisions for myself.

I wanted to change that. First, I put together a notebook of everything that was me. I created categories like "decorating" and "summer clothes" and cut pictures out of magazines of things *I* liked. What a concept. Two years later, I had my own little apartment all painted and decorated just the way I liked it and had a couple of closets worth of clothes that I chose. I was also working in television, which is something I had always wanted to do.

I remember deciding on Valentine's Day that I was ready to start dating again. In preparation of my return to the dating world,

I wrote out a "Cosmic Purchase Order" and on it listed all of the qualities I was looking for in a man. One of the items was "likes kids." Another item was "recovering danger boy." To me, that meant a guy who had a black leather jacket in his closet that he didn't much wear anymore. Some of the other things that were important to me were that he love music, *Star Trek*, camping, and animals. He had to be able to be vulnerable and open. Responsible, creative, and artistic wouldn't hurt, either.

I hung up this list in my office and added items whenever they occurred to me. I ended up with about twenty requirements on my wish list. He would be a tough man to find. But this was what I wanted.

Every Sunday morning I volunteered at my church as a camera-person. (They aired their weekly service on a local cable program.) One Sunday I was running a camera when I felt someone behind me. I turned around and had to catch my breath. Wow, there he was! This man was drop-dead gorgeous and reminded me of David Bowie. He was slender and graceful—and could he wear a pair of 501s. His eyes just sparkled. He was a fellow cameraperson, too.

The next day I got so scared that I tore up my Cosmic Purchase Order and flushed it down the toilet. Whenever I saw this new man, Steve, at church, I became brisk and businesslike. I knew if he got within five feet of me he would instantly know how I felt about him. If he walked into a room, I walked out of it. I guess I wasn't as ready to date as I thought.

Two months later I became the director for the church video team and was forced to call Steve to schedule him for duty. The simple question I posed to him on the phone was, "Can you work on Sunday?" Two hours later we said good-bye. We talked about

Star Trek, music, and movies. Steve was my Cosmic Purchase Order come to life.

A few days later, Steve called and asked me out. I told him I had to check my planner and would get back to him. Of course I ran into my coworker's office yelling, "He asked me out, he asked me out!" We watched the Fourth of July fireworks together and spent the whole afternoon at the park. He played songs for me on his guitar, and I read him passages out of my favorite books. We had our first kiss that night under the fireworks. I was thrilled, excited, and scared to death. The day was perfect, the sky beautiful, and the company fabulous. It was one of the most fun days of my life. I kept thinking, *So this is what a perfect date is like.* It was about darn time!

There was no question in my mind at all that Steve was the right man for me. He is a thousand times more special than I thought anyone could be. I had no idea that relationships could be so deep, meaningful, and joyous. Steve is everything in my life. To top it all off, he also has a black leather jacket in his closet.

Scott and Christie

bond trader, 32; teacher, 32

married May 29, 1993

❤

We met just a few days before college graduation. After classes ended we threw ourselves into Senior Week, which was basically one big drunken party. The climactic event of the week was the aptly named Booze Cruise, where basically everyone got trashed while we sailed around the Schuylkill River in Philadelphia. Unfortunately, I'd been elected designated driver that night by my roommates, so I was sitting up on the top deck of the boat by myself, away from the craziness. Out of nowhere, Christie came up, sat down next to me, and said, "I've had a crush on you for four years." I thought I was dreaming. I was psyched! I mean, this gorgeous woman had a crush on me, and, of course, my first thought was that I was going have a little fling during Senior Week. It was perfect. I guess Christie remembered me from a legal studies class we both took freshman year. I don't know why she liked me—I was the obnoxious guy in the back row. I never even knew who she was.

She was incredibly beautiful. We sat up there on the deck and talked the whole night, but there was no kissing. To complicate matters, she told me she had a boyfriend of three years who was also on the cruise with us. I think it was pretty clear she didn't care much about what he thought. When we all got off the boat, the boyfriend came up to Christie and said, "Come on, let's go home." And to my amazement, she told him, "No, I'm going home with Scott." My friends were really impressed. Hell, I was impressed. But I did the right thing that night and drove her right home.

Christie broke up with her boyfriend, and, a few days after the cruise, I took her to a baseball game at my old high school, which was really romantic. At least I thought so. Christie is such a natural, down-to-earth Midwestern girl. I liked everything about her—the fact that she played the violin and was so independent and very close to her family. This woman has been nothing less than a breath of fresh air in my life. My last week of college was the best one of all.

Kathy and Bruce

teacher, 51; editor, 53

married September 7, 1974

♥

$\mathcal{I}$ picked my husband up hitchhiking in Barcelona. My friend Lori and I had been driving around France and Spain one summer when I was twenty-one. This is what people did in 1969: they'd order their Volkswagens from the factory, go to Europe, and use them to travel around before shipping them back to the States. One day we were in Barcelona at the American Express office, waiting to pick up our mail. We'd told our friends and family to write us at various Amex offices in Europe. As we were standing there, we saw this fellow making his way down the line asking each person, "Are you going to Madrid?" People were turning him down left and right. Finally, he asked us if we were going to Madrid. We said no, we were going to Geneva. He did an about-face and announced, "Oh, I think I'll go there."

To this day, Bruce insists his plans were flexible. I, of course, know that he changed his entire itinerary to be with me. He was kind of pushy, no doubt. Lori and I thought, *Who is this guy?* We needed mull over whether we were going to give him a ride, so we told him we'd meet him back at the Amex office in an hour. We hadn't picked up any hitchhikers before, but Bruce was so persuasive. And it wasn't as if he was standing by the side of the road with his thumb out. Lori and I were kind of impressed when he told us he was a teacher. We just couldn't believe someone who looked about eighteen could be a teacher. We decided to take a chance on him.

When we got back to the meeting place, Bruce had someone else with him! Then we really thought he was a bit much. He was offering up Lori's hatchback to other random hitchhikers. Lori and I were such good sports about it all that we ended up taking them both, anyway.

On the ride to Geneva, I realized I was very physically attracted to Bruce. I thought he was quite handsome. He had a great sense of humor, and we had a lot of laughs during that car ride. Undoubtedly, Bruce was a very agreeable traveling companion.

It took us a few days to get to Geneva. One night Lori and I stayed in a hostel while Bruce slept outside in the car. He didn't want to spend the money. When we got to Geneva, Bruce posted a notice on the youth hostel bulletin board looking for someone to travel with for the next leg of his trip. I saw his note and told him that I'd like to hitchhike with him for a bit. My excuse was that you really meet so many more people that way than when you're traveling by car. I was interested in Bruce and he was not really making the first move so, hey, I figured *someone* had to. The two of us split off from Lori. Bruce and I headed to Milan and Florence and planned to meet up with Lori and some other friends a few days later.

By the time we got to Florence, our romance was in full swing. How could it not be in such a beautiful, sensual city? We strolled along the Arno River and walked up and down the quaint, winding little streets. We stayed in a wonderful pensionne and even shared a room—and not because we wanted to save money. Without our other friends around, things seemed suddenly different. Bruce stayed with me for the rest of his vacation. We traveled to Venice, Salzburg, Munich, Amsterdam, and Frankfurt. Eventually, he had to go home, back to Philadelphia. I went to visit Bruce once I arrived back in the States. Then I returned home to California.

We corresponded that first year and visited once or twice. The relationship continued to grow over time until we were so comfortable with each other that we knew we just didn't want to be with anyone else. After I tried living in his city, Bruce eventually moved in with me in California. At that time, single girls did *not* live with their boyfriends. My parents were shocked by the whole thing. They liked Bruce, but they really couldn't handle the living arrangements. Everyone told me, "He won't respect you and he'll never marry you after this!"

They were wrong. Now we have two grown daughters and even though I don't want them to give rides to strangers, I joke with them, "Be careful who you pick up hitchhiking, because you never know where it will lead! He may turn out to be your lifelong companion." Luckily, I picked up the right guy.

Andrea and Neil

mother, 30-something; investment banker, 30-something
married August 13, 1994

♥

*I*t was a warm summer night in New York City, and I was on my way home from work. I was walking up First Avenue when I realized I needed money for the next day. I debated going to the cash machine right then or waiting until morning, but since I'm always running late and in a rush, I thought I'd better take care of that errand right away. So I went into the Citibank on Seventy-ninth Street. After I walked out and was standing at the corner waiting for the light to change, I noticed an adorable guy next to me. He was so cute with his cleft chin and preppy clothes. His face was familiar to me, and I realized had seen him before around the neighborhood walking his dog. But we'd never met.

We looked over at each other and in an instant, our locked. His dog started jumping up, trying to grab someone else's pizza. The cute guy, Neil, then looked at me and said, "I didn't feed my dog today."

We talked as we walked uptown, and when we reached his apartment on Eighty-first Street, Neil invited me up to his place. As a single woman living in the Big Apple, I wasn't going into a stranger's apartment, even though he already felt like a friend. Plus, I noticed he had this blondish-white patch of hair on the back of his head. It reminded me of that cheesy eighties trend in which guys grew long tails off the back of their heads and bleached them blond. I'm pretty conservative and thought this guy might be a little weird. There was no way I was going into his apartment solo.

Instead of letting me walk away, Neil had his golden retriever do some pet tricks for me. It was little stuff, like getting the dog to hand him his paw. The dog wasn't jumping through hoops or anything. But I realized this guy was interested in me. It made me giggle to think that Neil was trying to impress me with his pet. He was doing anything he could to keep me there, talking to him. And I was swept away by the moment. It was a warm summer night, and here was this cute guy with a golden retriever who was trying to wow me. I was really flattered.

He asked me where I lived, which was just two blocks away, and he offered to walk me home. We ended up sitting on the steps in front of my brownstone for hours, chatting away. It was a very free-flowing, smooth conversation. There were no silences, no pauses. There was a tremendous connection between us. I loved his deep voice, and I was really attracted to him physically. But then we realized there was a big age difference between us. I was five years older! Instantly, I thought, *Oh, there went that one.* I really didn't think that anything could come of it after that.

Then Neil caught me off guard when he said bluntly, "You know I'm going to ask you out." I was surprised. I thought we'd be just friends and that he'd be too intimidated to ask an older woman out. He, however, thought nothing of it. We talked and talked until after midnight. The next night was our first official date. It was the most incredible evening of my life, and it only got better from there.

It was sheer fate that Neil and I bumped into each other on the street corner. Simply serendipitous. Dusty was the name of his dog, and I always say his name should have been Destiny because he brought us together.

Mitzi and Brent

mother, 35; media executive, 35
married June 18, 1994

❤

One night in January, a girlfriend dragged me to a black-tie fund-raiser. I was not in a social, flirty mood, and I was just really dreading this party. The guy I had been dating for five years had just moved to London, and we'd split up. The last thing I wanted was to meet other men. The day of the party, there was no getting my nails done, no primping. I threw on a black suit and tied a tight bun in my hair and went.

Of course the party was filled mostly with couples. My friend and I and another girl sat on a bench by the dance floor, watching everyone have a good time. It was a little pathetic. The two of them wandered off and I was happy to just sit there, not even trying to meet anyone or make an effort. All of a sudden, I saw two guys make a beeline for me. One was a short, dark-haired, guy who was doing some smooth dance moves. The other one was tall, tan, blond, and athletic looking. I was thinking to myself, *Ugh, here we go . . .* and wondering what kind of ridiculous line they'd try to use on me.

The short one dropped down on one knee and announced, "I'm Vince. Here's my business card." The other one plopped himself down next to me and said, "I'm Brent. I saw you first," and he whipped out his business card, too. I was completely disarmed. My mood turned around immediately, and I started to laugh because these guys were just too funny. They were sweet and cute and completely harmless. Their approach wasn't half bad. In fact, it kind of worked. I made a mental assessment of the two of them: Vince was very outgoing and coming up with lots of jokes. Brent, meanwhile, was my idea of a real Midwest hunk who must have been smart, since he went to Princeton. They were dying to leave this boring party and asked me to go dancing with them. Not in my wildest dreams did I think I was going to end the night by club-hopping with a couple of strangers! Still, they were great guys and the friends I had come with had left without me. I asked myself, *Why not?*

First we stopped at my apartment so I could change into jeans. Vince and Brent waited in the lobby for me for a long time while I debated whether I really wanted to go out with them or not. By the time I came downstairs, I expected them to be long gone. But they were there, still waiting patiently for me.

On our way to the club, I was thinking, *What am I doing?* Here I had known these guys for about an hour and I was running off to some crazy place with them at 1:00 A.M. But we had a great time. I would dance with Vince for a little while, then take a turn with Brent. It was all very friendly and nonthreatening. They both kept asking for my phone number, but I said no.

Toward the end of the evening, Vince said, "Look, I know you're going to pick my friend over me because he's the good-looking one and always gets the girls." He did have a point. If I had to choose one, it would have been Brent. He was much more my type. But these two were best friends, and the last thing I wanted to do was to come between them. I knew I couldn't date either one.

The cab dropped Vince off first and again he pressed his card into my hand. When we got to my apartment, Brent kissed me on the cheek. As I was shutting the door of the cab behind me, he made one last final effort to get my number. Exasperated, I told it to him quickly and said good night.

The next day, I felt so disappointed. I had just met the greatest man, but it was such a sticky situation. I had both the guys' phone numbers, but I knew I couldn't call either of them. A few weeks later, my phone rang and it was Vince, wanting to know why neither one of them had heard from me. Every day for two weeks, Vince called and pestered me to go out with him. After dozens of these calls, I finally agreed to a friendly cup of coffee with him. But when we got together, he told me he wanted us to be more than friends. I said that I just couldn't and that I was sorry.

Over the next several months, I kept looking at Brent's card sitting on my coffee table, thinking I should call him up and invite him to the ballet or to a play. I was such a chicken, I just didn't pick up the phone. And even though he lived only a half block away, we never ran into each other. In the meantime, I spent lots of time by myself, reading books. One Friday night six months later, I came home after a date to find the little red light blinking on my answering machine. I couldn't imagine who would be calling so late on a Friday night. The message said he wasn't sure if I remembered him, but we met a long time ago. It was Brent. He finally called!

On our first date Brent picked me up at my apartment, and

when I walked out of the elevator, I turned around and saw him. He was ten times more handsome than I had remembered. I was stunned. He was tall and cute and had a big bright smile. What had I been thinking all this time?

We went to a wonderful Italian restaurant and had a great time talking and laughing and ordering tons of food. I still remember to this day what he was wearing: a nice suit and a blue shirt trimmed with a white collar. He had such a fantastic body—even through his suit I could tell how muscular and slim he was. I remember looking at his left hand, which was beautifully tanned, and thinking it would look gorgeous with a wedding band on it. I know it's ridiculous, but it's true.

At the end of the night, he dropped me off at my apartment and kissed me good-bye. *Phenomenal.* When our lips parted, we both pulled away, looked into each other's eyes, and at the same time we both said, "Mmmm." It was utterly delicious. And then we kissed again for another five minutes. I was *this* close to asking him to come up to my apartment, even though it was just a first date. That's how great a kisser he was. It took every ounce of willpower to just say good night.

We had the most wonderful dates. I cooked him romantic dinners, which we ate on my tiny city terrace. He ate everything I made and loved it. Once he whipped up Vince's mother's special spaghetti sauce in his apartment. We rented movies and went swimming. One summer night we went out for Thai food and got caught in a torrential downpour while we were running home, which was very romantic. After only a few weeks, I was officially upgraded to girlfriend status. Then he delivered some bad news: in two months, he would be moving to London to take a new job with the family business.

What was it with London? I couldn't believe it. Maybe fate

just wasn't working on my side. We decided that until he left, we were going to have "Relationship Concentrate" and squeeze everything we could into those last few weeks. He called me every day, and we saw each other almost as often. Brent is so full of life: he loves to laugh, to work hard, to eat with gusto. He cares very much about family, and that was very important to me, too. We spent the most wonderful fall together. The whole time I kept kicking myself for having wasted all those months by not calling him.

Somewhere along the way, I asked Brent why it took him so long to get in touch with me. He and Vince had a pact, he explained. It was pretty rare that the two of them were ever interested in the same girl, but if they were, they took turns. Brent got first dibs on the last girl they had met at the same time, and when they met me, it was Vince's turn. The other rule was that if one guy made a move and nothing came of it, he had a six-month grace period with that particular girl. After that, she was fair game. I thought their strategy was really hilarious, but so dumb! What if Brent and I had forgotten about each other or fallen for someone else during that ridiculous waiting period?

Brent left for England in October and we still talked every day. Nothing had changed, and we were surprised that we still felt the same way about each other—head over heels. A few months later, he asked me to join him in Europe, to move there and live with him. It was a crazy idea. I'd have to quit my job, put all my things in storage, and dive into the unknown. We were both in sheer panic about the prospect, but I knew I had to give it a shot. I packed three suitcases and figured if it didn't work, I'd pack them right up again and catch a plane home. *What the hell*, I thought. *It's for love.* And from the second I stepped into Brent's London apartment and into his arms, it was wonderful.

Veronica and Will

promotional marketing executive, 32; software salesman, 38

married June 29, 1996

♥

Will and I met through my personal ad in *New York* magazine. It wasn't the first time I had placed or answered a personal, but it was his very first venture into this new world.

Will was at the dentist's office one weekday morning. Killing time in the waiting room, he leafed through some magazines and just for laughs, he insists, starting scanning though the personals. My ad read: "J. Crew blue-eyed swimmer, 29, seeks tall, handsome, athletic, educated man with wit, 34–40." Finally, the nurse called him in, and he tossed the magazine back on the reception room's coffee table.

Back in his car in the parking lot, Will couldn't stop thinking about my ad. He *had* to have that copy of *New York* magazine. The issue was a few weeks old and he had no choice but to steal it from the office. He gracefully went back in, casually threw his raincoat down on the coffee table, and went to use the men's room. Leaving the office once again, he skillfully scooped up both his raincoat and the magazine and was outta there.

Later that night, he wrote me a two-page letter. This man writes a great sentence. Will is witty and intelligent, and he wasn't into the usual dating games. He told me he was a former pro-baseball player and sent me a cute photo of himself. I was impressed.

I received a total of sixty-six responses to my ad, and Will's was the sixty-sixth. The night of our first date, I waited near the front door of the bar so I could check him out ahead of time through the window. I saw him sauntering toward the place, a big lumbering guy. There was no ice to break. The rest is a dream.

Physically and emotionally, he is exactly who I was looking for. I love his easygoing nature. (I am, by contrast, high-strung and constantly spinning.) I love that he makes and keeps friends easily and that friends and family are as important to him as they are to me. And I love the fact that even though he's honest, he had the wisdom to swipe that magazine from the dentist's office that all-important morning.

Marcia and Bedros

full-time mother, 40; architect, 42

married June 7, 1986

♥

$\mathcal{I}$t's quite possible that had I been a taller person, my husband and I would never have gotten together. I was studying in the Soviet Armenia as a foreign exchange student. On the day I moved into the dorms, it seemed like I was the only one there. The halls were nearly deserted. But as I was struggling to hang up my curtains, a couple of boys walked by. They looked in and saw that, at a mere five feet tall, I needed some help. One of them came in and helped me. The other, inconsiderate one kept walking. He was the one I later married.

Even though he didn't help me, Bedros knew where I lived. We were the only two people to move in that day. The dorms had sat empty all summer, and there was an awful mouse problem. Just terrible. Bedros invited me over to his dorm room that night so I wouldn't have to spend too much time in the company of rodents. He was studying art, so while I was with him for the evening, he drew a little sketch of me. And he gave me a tiny little nose, which wasn't exactly accurate. It was while we were debating the size of my facial features and I was teasing him about his artistic ability that he just slid over and practically laid down on top of me. It was an absolutely wild pass, and my instinctive reaction was to slap him. He was barely even deterred. As I stomped out of his room, he said, "There are going to be mice in your room. Wouldn't it be safer to spend the night here?" That was one offer I was able to refuse.

This guy was not just a jerk, he was the KING of jerks. He was the biggest idiot I had ever met. I had never been thrown back on a bed like that before. I couldn't comprehend how anyone could be quite so aggressive just hours after we met. When I went back to my room I was frazzled and undone. And then as I lay down in bed and turned out the lights, I heard a mouse chewing on something. Bedros was right about that, at least.

It was months before I could treat him like a normal person. As the school term went on, he did ridiculous things. As I would be leaving my room for dance class at 6:00 A.M., he'd bellow down the stairwells of the dorm, "Am I going to see you tonight?" Or he'd yell, "Put something nice on when you get home! I'm going to take you to a restaurant!" He would wake up the entire dorm with all this hollering.

After a while, his relentless pursuit started to become funny, and he no longer annoyed me like he once did. One day when he yelled out that he wanted to take me to dinner that night, I just said okay. I must have been in a strange mood that day.

We ate in a little restaurant that was actually tucked away in a wine cellar. It was very romantic to be nestled into a little booth with Bedros, swathed in candlelight. We ate tons of delicacies that were very hard to come by during the Soviet times. At the end of the night, we had cognac and champagne. I felt a flutter in my stomach, and it wasn't from the food.

Bedros was so attractive. He had soft curly hair that was just a little overgrown, and about a two-day stubble on his face. In his eye was a little-boy twinkle that let you know he was always up to something. That twinkle was what got me. And he had a quick laugh—just about anything made him chuckle. Part of his appeal was that he was so cocksure and just laughed the world off. Nothing got to him, and I liked that perspective on life. And God, was he charming. I guess that's why I thought he was such a jerk at first—he used that charm to try to take advantage of me that first night.

At the end of the year, it was time for me to return home. Bedros was staying to continue his work on a master's degree. I knew that I needed to leave and grow up a little bit, but I also knew Bedros was the one I was going to marry. We continued to date and many years later, we walked down the aisle together. I had to go all the way around the world to find my mate.

Eleanor and Danny

executive secretary, 59

married July 3, 1963

♥

$\mathcal{J}$t was August in the year 1962, and I was twenty-one years old. It was a time when girls ran in packs looking to meet guys, and for me the usual Friday night meant going to a dance club with my three friends Gladys, Joan, and Vivian. Gladys and I had similar taste in men, and therefore we tended to stay clear of each other. One evening when the three of us were out at a club, a young man whom I was not particularly interested in began talking to me. Before I could end the conversation, along came Gladys, who introduced herself and started to chat with this gentleman. I was furious! How did she know if I was interested in this guy? How dare she butt in on my turf! I vowed to get back at her.

And get back at her, I did. On Sunday of that very same weekend, we had all planned to head to a beach club in Spring Valley, New York, for singles-only day. I sat dangling my legs on the side of the pool and couldn't wait for the first guy to approach Gladys while she lay on a chaise longue poolside. I kept looking back at her, waiting to make my move. Along came my chance: a gentleman sat down on the edge of her chair.

Instantly I approached him and asked him if he would like to play Ping-Pong. Of course he said he'd love to. I was smashing in my bathing suit and far better looking than Gladys. His back had been toward me, but when he turned around and I looked at him for the first time, I was very pleasantly surprised. He was much better looking than the guy I met at the club that Friday night, and I immediately liked what I saw.

We spent the entire day playing Ping-Pong, swimming, and most of all getting to know each other. I found out that Danny was from the Bronx, where I lived, too. He was nine years older than I, which was great because I found older men to be much more mature. The fact that he owned his own trucking company showed me that he was stable and successful. We also had something out of the ordinary in common—the loss of our fathers.

We had lots of fun and shared many laughs that day. Eventually, the sun started to go down, and it was time to leave. Danny asked if he could take me home, and I happily agreed. Gladys, though, was concerned. "You barely know the guy," she said. I somehow felt that she was not looking out for my best interests. She was jealous that I met someone on this singles day and she did not. Regardless of what she thought, I felt extremely safe in Danny's hands. On the way home, we ended up parking the car and having a little make-out session, which was composed of kissing only. He was a great kisser. When he dropped me off, he promised to call.

The next day Danny phoned me, and we began a wonderful relationship. We dated during the week and spent every Saturday evening together, going to the movies or to dinner or double-dating. I even rode with him on his truck to make deliveries to his clients. Within a matter of months, we were an exclusive couple. The turning point in our relationship for me came during the holiday season that year. We spent Thanksgiving together and he planned New Year's Eve for us and took me to an elaborate catered party. I realized then that Danny could very well be the man I would marry.

My birthday was in January, and I was wondering what he would buy me for a gift. I knew what he chose would be very indicative of what he felt for me. I was pleasantly surprised when I received a beautiful watch. In those days, that meant he was making a serious commitment to me. We became engaged five months after we met and got married six months after that. Gladys remained jealous throughout our entire relationship, so I asked Joan to be my maid of honor at our wedding. Vivian moved out West, and we lost touch by the time Danny and I got married.

Danny and I spent twenty wonderful years together. When he passed away, not only did I lose my lover, husband, and the father of my children, but most of all I lost my best friend.

Diana and P. J.

entrepreneur, 29; internet product developer, 27

married February 19, 1997

♥

$\mathcal{Q}$uite ironically, it was my boyfriend who unwittingly introduced me to my future husband. I had been dating Bart, a Dutch guy, for three years. At the time it was the most serious relationship I'd ever been in.

Bart and I were president and vice president of the ski club at the University of Arizona. We'd organize trips to the Rocky Mountains, rent buses, and sign people up. One Thanksgiving, we took the club to Park City, Utah.

The first day we arrived, after a full day of skiing, we got together for après-ski drinks in the lodge. I asked Bart if he had a cigarette, and he said no. This guy next to me told me he had one. I remember so vividly turning around to speak to him and seeing my future husband for the first time. My stomach just turned over. I looked at him and I just knew. He was sitting with his back to this huge window that opened up to the mountain.

The light was coming in behind him, forming a little halo. His hair was all staticky and his eyes were so bright green.

I looked at him and thought, *Oh, my God, who is this guy?* I had never seen him before. I didn't notice him on the bus or at any of the meetings. I liked him immediately and was so attracted to him. Even though we'd hardly spoken, I knew this was the end of my relationship with Bart. *I've met somebody I need to be with,* I thought immediately.

Bart had promised skiing lessons to some friends, and the next day he went off to take some runs with them. It was actually Bart who suggested I ski with P. J., instead. I skied with P. J. all day and we hit it off immediately. I knew what my plan was—I wanted him. P. J., however, was acting really coy. I've since found out he was clued into the fact that I was interested in him. He was feeling it, too. But he was having a fun time playing hard to get.

Riding back to the condos that night on the bus, a girl from some other trip was hitting on P. J. It was driving me crazy, but of course I couldn't say anything. P. J. ended up getting off the bus and going to a party with her. I was furious, but since I was dating Bart, there was nothing I could say or do about it. P. J. knew all along what he was doing to me.

After the trip, I found a million excuses to be with him. I was wishing and hoping it would turn into something more than just friendship. But I had a big problem with cheating on my boyfriend. I wasn't going to have an affair behind his back and string both guys along. But at the same time I didn't want to go through the ordeal of splitting up with Bart if I was going to be rejected by P. J.

As soon as P. J. and I got together, I broke up with Bart immediately. I was over at P. J.'s apartment one night, sitting on his couch when he first kissed me. He swears I made the first move, but really, he did. It started out with his offering to give me a massage, and the next thing we knew, we were rolling around in bed together. We used a whole bottle of coconut oil. Everything that he owned ended up smelling like that oil for months. And I've never been able to smell coconut again without remembering that night.

P. J. was really daring. He was a rock climber and skier and a real risk taker. He was really popular with everyone and always had a group of guys hanging around him. He doesn't have an enemy in the world. People naturally flock to him. And I'm not like that. I probably repel more people than I attract. I'm really outspoken, and people take offense to things I say. P. J. on the other hand, is really kindhearted and sweet and soft-spoken. He's really nurturing. It's an extremely attractive quality and one of the reasons we get along so well. We make a good team.

Once I was free to date P. J. openly, our relationship became really intense. Everybody around us could feel it. We connected and anyone near us could sense what was going on. We couldn't keep our eyes or hands off each other. And we didn't want to be away from each other for even a minute.

I've seen Bart only once since I left college, and it was pretty awkward. Understandably, he was never too happy about who I ended up with.

The incredible thing is that I had been considering breaking up with him for a long time, but if we had stopped seeing each other even a month earlier, I wouldn't have been on that ski trip. And I never would have met my husband.

Clair and Eric

executive recruiter, 50-something; photographer, 50-something

married May 5, 1982

♥

I was at the point in my life when I was eager to meet someone, my special man. For about six months I had been thinking, *I'm ready, why aren't I meeting anyone?* So, every occasion I had to socialize and meet new people, I thought, *Maybe tonight . . .*

It was a July evening in 1979 when I met Eric. One of my friends had invited me to an art show at the World Trade Center, in New York City, where her work was on display. I looked forward to the evening, especially because I'd be among people who shared my interest in the arts. I wore my favorite green blouse and a flattering pair of slacks and looked great. With high hopes, I anticipated adventure that evening.

The show was in an enormous space. Everywhere I looked there were people sipping wine, munching on cheese and crackers, and looking at the paintings and sculpture. Eric, whom I later married, recalled the event as an anonymous occasion for viewing art and not at all intimate. There was so much going on—so many distractions and different things to look at—that it was all the more magical that we found our way to each other through the chaos.

Wandering around looking for a familiar face, I noticed a dark-haired, bearded man who for some reason seemed familiar. I looked at him and thought, *There's somebody I want to meet.* He was wearing shorts and clogs and had great knees. I was so attracted to his artistic look. Without thinking too much about it, I walked toward him, even though he was already talking to a woman. I thought, *Well, if I get my hand slapped, okay. I can handle it.* But it was such an informal night that it felt perfectly natural for me to join them and introduce myself. I can't say I was disappointed when the other woman wandered away. Eric and I got into a great conversation about the show, photography, and poetry. Eric was a photographer, and I was writing poetry then. Ironically enough, we discovered that the same artist, my sculptor friend, had invited each of us there that night. The more we talked, the more I liked him, and when it came time to leave, we took a train to Brooklyn together, since we both lived there.

When we got to our neighborhood, Eric suggested we have a drink, so we stopped at a café before he walked me home. I was very attracted to him physically. Plus, he was creative and grounded and had a strong sense of himself. I found him interesting and refreshing and different from the guys I usually went out with. We exchanged phone numbers and went our separate ways. Months later, he told me he didn't get a lot of sleep that first night. He was too excited about meeting me.

A few days later, Eric called and asked me out. On our first date, he took me with him to work on a location photo shoot in Westchester, New York. Later that day we had a picnic. It was really lovely.

About the time that we met, I was planning a vacation. All of my friends were occupied with new boyfriends or other things. So I asked Eric if he'd be interested in traveling with me, making it clear that I meant only as friends. He agreed to go on the trip and convinced me to keep an open mind about being just friends. I wasn't too worried about spending a vacation with him, because by then I already had a good sense of him and knew he'd be a good traveling companion. We kept our plans flexible, though, and agreed that if for some reason it didn't work out, we'd just separate and do our own thing.

By the time we left for our trip about a month later, everything had changed. Our relationship had turned into a romance. By then, I was immensely happy and excited. I was already falling in love with him.

Throughout our trip to London and Scotland, we were inseparable and became extremely close. We were sharing tight living quarters as well as lots of romantic moments as we saw the sights of Europe. Eric and I got along very well, and being together all the time felt just incredibly natural to us. Our trip truly helped solidify our passionate relationship. We were close to begin with, but after two weeks in Europe, that was it. When we returned home, I went to my apartment and he to his. But we talked on the phone constantly and couldn't bear to be apart. I started to spend much of my time at his place and very soon thereafter moved in. One thing just led to another, and our relationship progressed smoothly and easily, without a moment of ambivalence. It just happened.

Alison and Glenn

magazine editor, 44; newspaper editor, 46
married December 17, 1983

❤

*I*t was 1981, and I went to San Francisco for a job tryout at the *Examiner*. My first day in town, Glenn was assigned to take me out to dinner because we had both previously lived in Kansas City. His boss thought maybe we'd have something in common. We had both worked on the newspaper there—he was on the afternoon edition and I was on the morning. Maybe we crossed paths, but I didn't remember him at all. He told me later he had vaguely remembered me as being bookish and unattractive and complained to his friends about how he had to take me out on the boss's orders.

Once I got into town, I was dropped off at the *Examiner*. It was brutally hot, there was no air conditioning, and I was standing around in the newsroom in the heavy clothes I had been wearing in Chicago. I sat there, uncomfortably, for *hours*. Glenn was supposed to pick me up at 6:00 P.M., but he didn't arrive until

8:30. I was *furious*. The first thing I ever said to my future husband was, "Let's make this fast, I have to get to work early tomorrow." I was not happy.

Glenn took me to a little Italian place by the water. Within an hour, I was thinking, *My God, I could really fall in love with this guy.* It was a big turnaround, to say the least. He was just very kind and very charming. Meanwhile I was engaged to marry another man in the Midwest. Glenn and I had a great time that night, and I got a call at work from him the next day. He asked me if I wanted to go hiking in Marin County. I thought this was incredibly cool. We hiked the Dipsea Trail over Mount Tamalpais. It was just the most beautiful scenery I'd ever seen in my life, and the romance of the day made me fall for him even more.

I told Glenn about my fiancé, and I wisely broke off that engagement very quickly. I told my fiancé that I met someone else, and he was very gracious about it.

I stayed in a motel for a few days, and by the following weekend I was staying with Glenn. Luckily, I got the job I was applying for and moved to San Francisco two weeks later. I had all of my stuff shipped out, and I planned to look for an apartment, but in the meantime I was living at Glenn's. Just temporarily, of course. If it didn't work out between us, I would find another apartment. My friends were thinking, "Well, here we go again . . ."

It wasn't long before Glenn called up his buddies and told them we moved in together. His best friend was so excited that Glenn had met someone that he just showed up in our bathroom one day while I was in the middle of the shower and cheerfully yelled out, "Glad to meet you!"

We kept our relationship a secret from our coworkers at the paper, and the funny thing was, a lot of them tried to set us up together. I always just said, "Nah, he's not my type!"

Mathew and Andrea

graphic artist, 45; makeup artist, 40

married August 30, 1980

♥

On vacation in New York City for a week, I made plans to drive out to my friend Marty's place for dinner one night. This was in 1979, and I was driving a Cadillac. So you can just imagine how enormous that car was. Marty lived on an extremely busy street on Long Island, and the first good sign was that I found a parking spot right in front of his building. It was a good omen.

But when I got to the building, Marty and his wife weren't home. It was a little odd, because they knew I was coming. I had been waiting in the lobby for a few minutes when a beautiful girl who was dressed to the nines walked up to the front door. She buzzed someone who didn't answer, so I let her into the lobby, too. I was brought up with manners. I couldn't let a woman wait outside. She took the elevator upstairs, then came back down. Then she walked up to me and said, "If you've traveled a long distance to visit someone and they're not home, what would you do?" It was the perfect opening. "Sit down and talk to a stranger," I said.

Andrea was so absolutely beautiful. She was all made up, wearing pearls and a fancy mauve outfit. We sat and talked in the lobby for a good hour. She told me what she did for a living. I told her I lived in California. I remember she had a clear pocketbook. I'd never met a woman with a see-through pocketbook before. I thought that was illegal. Andrea was also crocheting a blanket for her father as we sat and talked.

Eventually, Andrea mentioned that she was waiting for her sister, Saunda. My friend Marty is married to Saunda! The whole time, we had been waiting for the same people.

Finally, Marty and Saunda came home. They had gone shopping and it just took them forever. They had neglected to mention to me that they were inviting someone else over for dinner, but they really weren't trying to set me up with Andrea. It was very nice to have a very pretty girl there to talk to during the evening. Marty put on some romantic music, and we all drank too much wine. By the end of the evening, there was no way Andrea and I were driving home. We made the best of the foldout couch in their one-bedroom apartment. It was so stereotypical: she slept under the covers, and I slept on top. My parents brought me up right. One thing you never do is take advantage of a drunken woman. Besides, she never would have married me if I did.

The next morning, I said good-bye and gave her a peck on the cheek. Later that day, she called my parents' house on Long Island, where I was staying, and asked them, "Can Mathew come out and play?" She's not exactly shy. I was only in town for a week, so I didn't even think that we would see each other again. But I was wrong: we were together every day that week. We shared bottles of wine together and went to the movies. I was instantly attracted to her, and I knew I liked her. She was so much fun and very alive. There are no words for it; something was just right about us. Neither of us was looking for it, which is the best thing. I wasn't even interested in dating before I met her.

We had one official date that week when we went out to dinner. Andrea was a disaster. She spilled a glass of water and dropped a piece of butter. She was really nervous! Oh, she was cute and so funny. In so many ways, though, we were very different. She is very bold and I am normally very quiet. She's a night person, I'm morning. She likes shopping and I don't. She didn't like to exercise, but I did. But none of that mattered. To quote Andrea: We fit good.

Soon after we met, we realized that our paths had already crossed, not too long before. A month before my trip to New York, I had called Marty to tell him I was coming into town, and Andrea was the one who answered the phone at his apartment. We flirted with each other and, jokingly, I asked her if she wanted to come to visit me in California. I didn't know who she was, and I was just in a good mood. I heard her mother in the background yelling, "No! You're not going to California!" And her father yelled, "Only if there's a ring." But we didn't even exchange names.

The other strange coincidence was that our mothers had met completely by chance. Her mother sold cosmetics in beauty parlors and my mother came into one of her salons one day. Andrea's mother told my mom about her single daughter living at home. My mom went on and on about her unmarried son in California. Andrea's mother said, "Don't introduce them. My daughter's not going to California!" And then a short time later we met, anyway.

I didn't date anyone else after I met Andrea. Once I got home to California, we talked on the phone constantly. (While we talked, she'd be crocheting that same blanket she was working on the first day I met her.) It didn't take long before she started in with the "where is this going?" speech, and I knew she was as serious as I was. That's when our relationship really took off. One day, she called me at work and blurted out, "Let's get married." She really caught me off guard. But I smiled all day thinking about what she had said. We were married within ten months of our first meeting. To this day, I turn around every so often and ask her to marry me, because I never got the chance.

There's never a dull moment in my life with Andrea. For both of us, there's something relaxing about being together. A lot of times I know what she's going to say before she says it. We love to hold hands, and we're always touching each other. Even if we're in a quiet room doing nothing, we just like to be together.

We joke now about how we were destined to come together. Somewhere, there must have been writing on the wall. The strange thing is that many years before, Marty and I had fallen out of touch. We reconnected on the very last day before I moved to California. And if that hadn't happened, I never would have been at his apartment the night Andrea was there. Oh, and her dad never got that crocheted blanket she was working on the day we met. It's lying on the foot of our bed, nineteen years later, and it isn't going anywhere.

Sevina and Jeff

PR coordinator, 32; communications manager, 32
married March 23, 1996

♥

Some people say you can't find true love in cyberspace, but Jeff and I are living proof that you can. I knew there was no way I was going to meet anyone in the real estate office where I worked. And the bar scene is just not for me. People were always telling me about how many friends they met on-line and so I decided to post a personal ad on the web. Why not?

The problem with ads, though, is that you have just one shot to attract someone's attention. I thought that the people responding might feel just as awkward and uncomfortable as I did about it. To make things easier, I wrote a short description of myself and posed three questions for people to answer as creatively and honestly as they chose. I titled it: "I Want to GRAB Your Attention."

The first question was: "After a long week of work, you are looking forward to a glorious weekend, but awaken Saturday morning to find the skies full of rain. What do you do?" The answers I got ranged from rolling over and going back to sleep, teasing me awake to make love, and pulling out a guitar to strum along with the rain's natural rhythm. Then there was my future-sweetheart's response: enjoying hot Orange Zinger tea while reading a book beside the open window to enjoy the fresh breeze.

Next I asked: "If I could prepare your favorite meal, what would it be?" Some men hoped I could perfect their mother's famous hamburger casserole. (Gee, how romantic.) Others wanted to wine and dine me with an eight-course meal. Jeff was the only one to say that it didn't matter what we ate, as long as there was somebody special alongside him.

My last question: "You've discovered the secrets of invisibility. What do you do with your newfound powers?" Ninety-eight percent of the men, in one way or another, wanted to sneak into the women's locker room. My knight-in-shining-armor, however, said that he would miss the companionship of his friends too much to want to be invisible.

My ad brought about eighty responses, but I knew the moment I read Jeff's heartfelt e-mail that he was the one. From our very first correspondence, I thought things were going to be serious between us. His answers were perfect and unique. Jeff's e-mail was the only one that made me feel good all over, that made me feel good about the possibility of us. I fell for him immediately.

We started e-mailing back and forth, which was a real effort for me because I had to drive thirty minutes after work to use my friend's computer. But it was more than worth it. Each day, we wrote each other and told each other about our backgrounds and our hopes and dreams. He would send me the lyrics to Eric Clapton songs that I loved. There was definitely some flirting going on. One day he wrote that he missed me, and that just lit me up inside. I finally met someone whom I really really liked. I remember telling people that I had found a guy who was really different.

One night he emailed me his photo and I was really nervous. The picture came up a bit at a time. I couldn't stand it! My palms were sweaty. I was thinking that this could make or break the deal. Maybe one unknown part of me would rear its ugly head and insist that looks *are* important. He looked exactly as I thought he would—perfectly adorable. Warm feelings floated through me. The following day I sent him a picture of me.

While we were e-mailing, Jeff tried to give me his phone number, but I wanted to take things really slow. After about three weeks though, I got up the nerve to talk to him on the phone. The first time I heard his voice, I was nervous and exhilarated at the same time. I was flustered trying to find the right words to say. But after a few minutes, we both relaxed.

We starting talking on the phone all the time and the e-mailing fell by the wayside. Jeff seemed to really care about me and about how my day was. He always found a way to cheer me up if I was feeling down. I appreciated his sense of humor, but most of all I loved him for his raw honesty. I thought, *Oh my God, this is a real person here.* He was not afraid to show me his true self.

When we finally met in person, it felt like a blind date. Things just were not the same. We were both very shy and reserved with each other. But after a few hours, our nerves calmed, and we relaxed a bit. It started to feel more like it did all those hours we spent flirting with each other on the phone. Throughout the date, Jeff was very attentive, always watching me and holding my hand. I felt cherished. At the end of the night we gave each other a quick peck on the lips, which was perfect because it made me want more. In the end, I got a whole lot more—the husband I always dreamed of.

Jim and Sheri

information systems manager, 30; tour services coordinator, 30

married June 5, 1999

♥

I was hung over and tired on the flight home to New York after a vacation in Santa Barbara. But at least one thing was going my way: I got a seat in the exit row, so I had some extra leg room. During boarding, a flight attendant came over to me to read me the FAA disclosure about helping out in an emergency. And she was striking.

Before boarding I had picked up a few bottles of mineral water, and I asked the flight attendant for a bottle opener. Passengers were still finding their seats, and it was really hectic. But still, she was kind enough to go back to the kitchen to hunt down an opener for me. By the time she got back, I had realized that my bottles had twist-off caps. Oops. I was not exactly making points with her right away.

The last night of my vacation, my friends and I had gone out partying, so I had quite a headache that day. I was tired and not feeling too courageous at all. There were tons of people on the flight, and I didn't want to blatantly hit on the stewardess. I'm just not that type of guy.

My stroke of luck, though, was getting an exit row seat. On this 747, there were two flight attendant seats facing my row, and the cute one sat in one of them. While talking to the guys on either side of me, I mentioned where I was working. The flight attendant, Sheri, suddenly broke into our conversation and asked me if I happened to know Donna, who also worked for my company. It just so happened that Donna was a really good friend of mine. She had actually trained me when I was first hired, and we had become pretty tight. Sheri told me she was Donna's cousin. I had heard Donna talking about her cousin all the time, but she never mentioned her by name.

We talked most of the six-hour flight to the East Coast. I was definitely attracted to Sheri. She was friendly, and judging from the job she chose for herself, I knew she had a taste for excitement and adventure. That was important to me. I love to travel, and she obviously did, too. I was pretty excited by the whole prospect of asking her out.

This was my strategy: after the plane landed and I was collecting my stuff, I asked her if there would be any cabs at the airport. She said sure but offered to give me a ride to Long Island as far as Long Beach. I wasn't going to Long Beach, but I would have taken a ride anywhere with this girl. Then I think she thought, *Wait a minute, this isn't the best idea*, and she quickly changed her mind. I didn't blame her at all. Plus, my parents were picking me up at the airport. If I'd had a chance to leave with Sheri, though, I would have just walked right past them. See you later, Mom! Instead, Sheri and I said good-bye. I mentioned something about getting together with Donna for happy hour sometime, leaving the door open for us to see each other again.

After I got home, I told everyone that I met a woman and that Sheri and I were going to be together for a long time. I knew as soon as I started talking to her that she was the one for me. I called up my friend who I had vacationed with in California and said, "I just found her!" He didn't believe it, but I was really sure. Something inside told me.

I was extremely confident about us from the beginning, from the moment I saw her. Sheri is probably the funniest person I've ever met. She's got the best repertoire of jokes. Anyone in her presence is drawn to her because she makes everyone feel good. Her outlook on life is another thing I love about her. She's really positive. No matter how bad things are, she looks at the silver lining. Nothing really fazes her.

The whole thing was really wild. When we started dating, we realized she knew a lot of the people I worked with. It's possible we could have met some other time, we just never did. Instead, we were thrown together on a random cross-country flight. If my friend hadn't been living in Santa Barbara, I wouldn't have been on that plane. Had I not been sitting in the exit row, I probably never would have seen Sheri or struck up a conversation with her. And if I hadn't been looking for the cheapest flight, I wouldn't have been on that airline at all. A lot of things had to happen in order for me to be there at that moment. With all these coincidences, it was definitely destiny.

Stephanie and Tom

mother, 36; lawyer, 37
married May 13, 1989

♥

Tom was my forbidden fruit. My friend Nina told me that under no circumstances could I date him, so that's exactly what I did. I hate to admit it, but as soon as she made this pronouncement, I was intrigued by Tom that much more.

Nina had a crush on Tom's roommate, Ken, so the four of us hung out quite a bit. Nina dragged me along so her eyelash batting and flirting with Ken wouldn't look quite so obvious. I had no idea there was anything brewing between me and Tom. I kept thinking how wonderful it was that guys and girls could be just friends like we all were. Little did I know that Tom had been telling his family he was in love with me for months.

Nina had other plans for Tom, though. She had decided that because he was so sensitive and caring, he was just perfect for her friend Diana, a sweet, quiet little thing. She had her little pea head set on it!

But Tom had a different idea. Later I found out he had been writing me unsent letters, which he read to his family. They were very romantic little notes that said "I think I'm in love with you. I think we should be together." His mother and sisters all yelled, "AACK! Throw them away!"

It took him a month and a half to screw up the courage to ask me out. The night we were to have our first date, I was also invited to my history professor's house for a potluck dinner. Since I wasn't doing too well in his class, I thought I'd better show up. Tom was a great sport about tagging along. When we walked in the door, everyone yelled, "TOM!" Tom, as it turns out, was the president of the history club. Even my professor was thrilled to see him. In this new setting, I saw Tom in such a different light. He was so outspoken and popular and intelligent. Suddenly, I had a whole new respect for him.

During those early months we were obsessed with hiding our budding relationship from Nina. We were continually sneaking around, which I have to admit really added to the fun. We couldn't go to any of our usual hangouts, like the old baked potato place, so we went into Sacramento and San Francisco. We had to be very clever and secretive, staying far away from campus.

Those first few weeks, Tom showered me with love letters and flowers. Once, when I was sick, he sent me a ficus tree. The card read, "May our love grow as does this tree." He was so sweet.

Eventually, Nina discovered our secret romance. One day I was supposed to be at the library, and she discovered my car in front of Tom and Ken's apartment. I was all cozied up with Tom when she came storming in. Was she mad! But that just made it all the better. The irony is that now she takes full credit for pairing us. And in a way, she's right.

Beth and Josh

student and mother, 32; investment baker, 36
married February 6, 1993

♥

When I first met Josh, there were two big problems that could easily have prevented our relationship from ever coming to life: his terrible shoes and his awful shaggy hair.

I was a waitress, working the dinner shift on Mother's Day, 1991. An attractive guy happened to come in with his mother and father and sit at one of my tables. The restaurant was packed, and I had really neglected them. Meanwhile, all of my gay waiter friends had quickly decided that this was the man I should be dating. They kept telling me how good he would be for me. They were giving me serious grief about it. I was instructed, "You go over to table two, and you talk to that nice boy there. Go get him."

Walking over to their table, I had a big, stupid smile on my face. I was grinning at him the way you do at someone you really like. Except that I didn't yet realize how attracted I was to him.

He didn't say very much to me, just asked a few questions about the wine and the southwestern steak. His mother, on the other hand, was asking me all about myself. "What do you do? What are you studying in school?" Later I learned that she said to Josh, "There's a nice girl. Why don't you ask her out?" His response was: "Please stop, Mom." I mean, who wants your mother to pick out a woman for you to date?

I gave this guy the once-over. When I got down to his shoes is when it all fell apart. He was wearing natural-colored leather loafers—a big, bad thing in my book. Of all the things he could have been wearing, I can't think of anything worse than natural loafers. I should preface this by explaining that my previous boyfriend was the worst dresser. I make this confession at the risk of sounding terribly shallow, but in all honesty, I just didn't want to dress anybody any more. I wanted a date who came predressed. I was willing to compromise on almost anything, but not that.

If he had walked out of the restaurant and I'd never seen him again, I probably wouldn't have given him another thought. A couple of hours later, though, I got a call at work. It was Josh. I was surprised to hear from him, but not completely shocked. He reminded me who he was, but how could I forget him and his shoes! He said, "I don't know if I'm out of line but I wanted to ask you to lunch." I was flattered and I reassured myself that he seemed normal and had nice parents. Usually the men who tried to pick me up at the restaurant were a little odd. I figured a meal with this guy couldn't hurt.

We had a nice time at lunch, but Josh was very distracted because he was a corporate attorney in the middle of his workday. The fact that he was a lawyer was a big minus for me. At the time, I was only interested in creative, artistic, bohemian types. He was much too corporate for me. Thankfully, Josh was wearing better shoes this time—black with buckles—but we still had a problem: he looked as if he hadn't had a haircut in six months. It was scraggly and pretty bad. Josh was very nice and had the potential to be cute, but I was pretty indifferent about the whole prospect. After the lunch date, my world was not rocked.

He phoned me a few times after that and I would return his calls when I knew he wasn't at home. My friend Diane kept telling me I was crazy for not pursuing him. She pointed out that here was a nice lawyer with a good job and some stability, unlike most of the men I dated. One day he called me while I was on the phone with Diane and I lied and told him I couldn't talk. I was on the phone long distance, I claimed. It's a big joke between us now. Whenever I say "long distance," that means from Greenwich Village to about Seventy-second Street! Diane insisted I return his call right away. Josh always tells me now that if I waited five more minutes to phone him back, I would have lost my chance with him for good.

We spoke for a long time that night. It was just an amazing phone call. He was so easy to talk to. To my surprise, he was very funny and charming. At the end of our conversation, he asked me, "Are we ever going to go out?" Suddenly, I really wanted to see him again. A major land shift had occurred during the course of this one call. Josh suggested dinner on Monday or Tuesday. Instinctively, I replied, "Monday's no good for me, maybe Tuesday." Of course I had absolutely nothing to do on Monday night. I don't know where this response came from. We agreed on Tuesday night at 8:30.

I was so cool about the fact that he was stuck at work and couldn't pick me up until 10:00 P.M. A lot of women might have had a problem with that. I believe that was really important in our relationship because he was always so busy at work, and I think he needed a woman who wasn't going to flip out every time he was late. When he arrived at my apartment, I was in for a major surprise: he had gotten his hair cut! He was dressed in a great Armani suit and looked *so* handsome! I was very excited. Suddenly, I was a little nervous. We had had that great phone call, and the shaggy hair was history. All the pieces were falling into place.

I always joke that once I found out he was really a bad guy gone good, I was hooked. He wasn't just an uptight corporate guy in a suit. There was a sensitive side of him that I discovered that night. It was a real treat to find someone who was not only stable and reliable, but artistic and creative as well. He was perfect: a mix of everything I could ever want in a person. I was smitten. After that night, there was no going back.

We really weren't as different as I had thought. And when he told me he always wanted to live in the city instead of the suburbs, I was captured. This was music to my ears. Of course we have our differences. In our relationship, he's the more solid half, the one with his feet planted firmly on the ground. I'm a little bit more free spirited. He's very calculated, whereas I like to rush into things. But I think we've had a positive influence on each other. We complement each other perfectly.

Alice and John

retired real estate broker, 94
married December 31, 1938

♥

*I*t was 1936 and I was thirty-one years old. At the time, I was married to a man named James. But we were separated because he was an alcoholic. I decided to go on a trip around the world with my friend Ruth to figure out if I was going to go back to James, or maybe go back to someone else. (I *cannot* divulge who that was!) At that time, it was unheard of for two women to travel alone. We took a ship from Canada, and it took five days to reach Honolulu, the first stop in our three-month itinerary.

We were peppy to go out the very first night in Hawaii, so Ruth and I joined up with our friends who lived there, Ken and Nona. We went to the Rathskellar, a place that Bing Crosby made famous. It was a bar in a basement and there was slow music with Hawaiian guitars. A friend of Ken and Nona's brought John to the Rathskellar that night. I was taken with him. He danced well, that was the main thing. I had a great time twirling around the dance floor with this man John.

The next time I saw John was when he came over to Ken and Nona's for cards. That first night he had bragged about how well he played bridge. He was a big bunch of *bull* and couldn't play worth a damn! But he was cute and fun, and I guess the bridge didn't matter too much because a romance started up pretty much right away.

Immediately, I decided to stay in Honolulu and give up the trip. John was a big part of that decision. But mostly it was because I was just free as a bird. I had given up my job and didn't have to worry about James anymore. He was a darling husband except for the drinking. So one of the things that appealed to me about John was that he was so serious. And that's what I wanted.

I filed for a divorce from James. He found out about my decision when he was served with the papers. Then the phones really started ringing. He cried, "You simply can't do this!" When I look back on it, I don't think the way I handled it was very considerate.

My romance with John wasn't so whirlwind because we knew we had to wait two years for my divorce to become final. But we saw each other *a lot*. Especially when he got his own little place on the beach in Waikiki. It was absolutely marvelous. We went out dancing constantly. I was insane about music. Absolutely bonkers. At the time I was living in a girls' hotel where no men were allowed, so we would spend time at his place. In the mornings I would scoot home just before they unlocked the doors at the hotel and I would make up a story, saying, "I've just been out for the most wonderful walk!" And everybody bought it.

John and I got married on New Year's Eve of 1938, as soon as the divorce was final. We got a judge to perform the ceremony even before the final seven-day waiting period was up. It had already been two years, and we just couldn't wait any longer! It was a tiny, beautiful ceremony at the minister's house on the water, overlooking the city. I wore dozens of tiny white leis. We were madly in love.

Because of all his drinking, James died at a very young age. And the other man in my life who I was involved with before my trip to Hawaii went on to marry a wonderful woman who adored him. Everything worked out just as it should have.

Sarah and Marshal

attorney, 33; doctor, 38

married March 5, 1994

♥

One day when I was twenty-four, I woke up on the wrong side of the bed. Or maybe it was the right side. I didn't like where my life was heading: getting married to the man I'd been dating for nine years, having 2.5 kids, and living in the suburbs of Johannesburg, South Africa. I'd had it: I was leaving everything behind and moving to America.

Everyone thought I was crazy. My mother thought I had lost my marbles and didn't think I'd actually go through with it. I had never been to America before and never even *wanted* to go. But for some reason, I knew I had to change my life drastically, and, somehow, America was the place to do it. My boyfriend in Johannesburg told me if I left not to bother coming back. Ours was a dead-end relationship, and he was a big reason why I needed to leave. I packed one tiny suitcase, told him good-bye, and took off.

In my mind, New York was Gotham city—the worst place in

the world. Surely it was filled with nothing but cockroaches and criminals. I was convinced I'd have to wear a money belt instead of carrying a purse. But how could I go to America and not see New York? It was practically obligatory. So I planned to go there for just four days and then tour around and see the rest of the country.

It was on the plane that it hit me. *What am I doing?! Where am I going?* I didn't know anyone and hadn't made any plans. When I stepped off the bus at Grand Central Station, I walked outside with my suitcase and stood watching in amazement the chaos around me. All those cars! All those people! For two hours, this little girl from South Africa sat on the sidewalk, staring at the insanity of the city and wondering what to do next.

Then I remembered one of my old childhood friends, Anthony, lived in New York. He wasn't particularly thrilled about my showing up out of the blue, but he agreed to let me stay with him for a few days. Anthony and his girlfriend, Donna, were kind enough to invite me to a barbecue Donna was having at her apartment. I was just hanging out with them at her place, when in swaggered one of Donna's roommates, Marshal, who was also South African. He was wearing nothing but a towel around his waist and had bulging muscles and a hairy chest. He thought he was hot stuff! I thought he was completely arrogant and had an attitude problem. I couldn't figure out why this guy rated himself so highly. I ignored him the rest of the night.

Anthony helped me get a temp job in his office for a few weeks. By this time, I realized that not only was New York not as bad as I thought, but I really loved it. So I thought I'd postpone my traveling for three weeks, take this little job, and then continue on my way. Anthony arranged for me to rent Donna's room in her apartment, since she didn't even live there full time. I moved in, and Marshal, the obnoxious guy, became my new roommate. What a nightmare.

Marshal was a terrible womanizer, just terrible. He was always out picking up girls, getting phone numbers and partying. But the funniest thing happened. As soon as we got to know each other a little and spent some time talking, I realized I'd been wrong about him. He was quite sweet, actually, and not arrogant at all. And he was extraordinarily funny. We laughed about the most ridiculous things until our bellies ached. He and I would go out together at night and end up talking for hours and hours. We told each other about our childhoods, our philosophy on life, our love lives—you name it. It was almost as if I already knew him. It usually takes years and years to form a solid friendship, but with Marshal, it was like all those years were squashed into one week.

We weren't, however, going to cross the line. I was just getting out of a nine-year relationship, and the last thing I wanted was to dive right into another one. Marshal, meanwhile, knew that for him, the hunt was everything. As soon as he slept with someone, that was it—he wasn't interested anymore. And things were so great between us, neither one of us wanted to ruin it.

One night I was out on a date with some guy, and suddenly I could not bear to be with this person one second longer. I didn't want to be with any human being other than Marshal. It was a blinding realization! I ran all the way home, bolted into the apartment, and found Marshal in bed sleeping. I jumped on him, woke him up and told him about my revelation with a sweetly planted kiss. We kissed passionately for ages that night. And I don't think he minded a bit that I interrupted his good night's sleep.

My three weeks were soon up, and my job was supposedly over, but I kept extending my stay again and again. I'd leave and do a bit of traveling and then come back to Marshal. After six months,

I needed to leave the country because my visa was expiring. I had plans to go to Europe, return to South Africa for a bit, and after that, I wasn't sure what I was going to do. As I was leaving, Marshal devastated me by saying that if I was going to come back to America, it couldn't be because of him. He didn't want to be a factor in my decision, and if I returned, it had to be solely my choice. I was furious and hurt.

Two days before I left, Marshal changed his mind. "Please come back," he told me. "I don't care what your reasons are. I just want you here." Everyone says a leopard doesn't change his spots, but this one did. It turned out he had stripes after all.

We did everything backward: We lived together before we made love and we got married before we got engaged. We had a quickie wedding in Las Vegas in a tacky little chapel. Then we announced our engagement in South Africa. And a year later, we got married again, properly this time.

Ours is a relationship that we both fought, that neither one of us wanted to be in. But we couldn't help it, because we belong together. Marshal's biggest gift to me is that he has brought joy and laughter back into my life. We had a connection that neither of us ever had before. We look at each other and know exactly what the other is thinking. I pick up the phone to call him and he's on the other end. We're like one unit with two bodies. I had to go to the opposite end of the world to meet my soulmate. My very first day in America, I found my husband.

Beth and Mark

mother, 36; salesperson, 38

married April 4, 1992

♥

$\mathcal{M}$y older sister always told me that someday I would meet my white knight. He was out there somewhere, she promised. His horse just must have gotten lost along the way! I wanted to believe her, but that man just never came along.

Some single friends of mine who were dating and looking decided to run personal ads in a magazine. It was the very "in" thing to do at the time. Of course, I was dying to see their ads, so I got a copy of the magazine and flipped through it to find theirs. Purely by chance, I came across one that read, "White Knight Looking for Princess . . ." Could this be my white knight?

I had never ever answered a personal, but this was just too good to pass up. Something told me I had to write to this man. My letter was short. I told him about myself and where I went to school, my hobbies and interests and enclosed a picture of myself.

I put it in the mailbox and promptly put it out of my mind. Several weeks later, I got a call at work. It was him. He had a very nice, distinctive voice. He asked me if I'd like to meet for drinks, and I did.

He recognized me from my photo, but I had no idea what he'd look like. I was not at all disappointed when I first saw him. Mark is very handsome, and I could tell just from looking at him that he's a good person. I really liked his sense of humor and his manner. Even though we hadn't planned to, we decided to go to dinner afterward. Things were moving along between us. I was sure I wanted to spend more time with him. After dinner, I was really touched that he found me a cab and made sure I was safely on my way home. So many men just leave you on a corner to fend for yourself in New York City! Mark was so gentlemanly and chivalrous.

My sister knew it was a good date because I wasn't home in a half an hour, like I usually am when I'm out with a real dud. I didn't know if I was going to hear from Mark again, but if I did, I was going to say yes to whatever he suggested for a second date. No pretending I'm too busy. No playing games. He called me three days later to ask if I wanted to share a picnic with him at an arboretum outside of the city. It was a beautiful place with acres of lawns and open fields and shady trees. I was a little nervous and didn't quite know what to expect, so I packed my Walkman, about eight magazines, and a towel. What did I know? I think he was a little disappointed when he thought we'd spend the afternoon talking to each other and I pulled out a library's worth of reading material. To this day, his father teases me and says, "You brought novels and a Walkman? I would have dumped you right away after the picnic!"

Luckily, Mark didn't do that. We held hands that afternoon as we strolled though the fields and shared our first kiss. I knew even early on that he could be the one.

It was a while before I told him about how I'd been looking for my white knight and that's why I answered his ad. I could tell from what he'd written that he believed in happy endings. And that's exactly what we've got.

Patty and Aria

film producer, 47; home builder, 46
married February 9, 1990

♥

$\mathcal{M}$any years ago, I was married to another man, Sam. During our entire marriage he always wanted to go to Israel and I refused every time. One of the reasons I resisted was that somehow I just knew that going to Israel would be an emotional experience that would change my life in ways I couldn't even predict. And I simply wasn't ready for that. Each year this issue would surface, and it added a lot of tension to our relationship. It turned out I was right. When I first ventured to Israel, I met the love of my life who saved me from impending disaster in more ways than one.

At the time, I was working as a film producer. Given the task of heading up ten fairy-tale movies for my company, I had hired all the directors and writers and lined up all the big-name actors. The only thing I was missing was a location, so for a year I scouted sites in Budapest, Prague, Spain, and Italy. Since these were fairy-tale movies, the only things I needed were a forest and a castle.

One day, the president of the film company called me up and said, "I want you on a plane in three days. We're doing all of these films in Israel." Now, Israel is the *only* place on earth that doesn't have castles or forests! It made absolutely no sense. Then I had to go home and face Sam. Our marriage had many cracks in it already, and the year I had just spent on the road did nothing but add to the strain. Sam stared at me and said, "You're going to Israel for your job when you've refused to go with me for years?" My answer was yes. These movies were *my* project and my big shot at success in the business. And it all came down to my going to Israel. My husband gave me an ultimatum: if I went, he would divorce me. Hysterical, I fought the Israel decision tooth and nail with everybody at my company. My boss told me if I didn't go, they'd fire me. In the end, I got on the plane and I went.

When I got to the set in Israel, the staff refused to talk to me. Not a word. I couldn't figure it out. The only person who would speak to me was the executive producer, who ran the studios in Israel. I didn't want to have anything to do with this guy, Jacob. But he was very friendly and told me not to worry, that the crew just didn't like Americans, and they'd get used to me. For two weeks this silent treatment continued. I called up my husband crying and he hung up on me. I was very nervous that all the directors and actors were going to show up in Israel and I wouldn't have any control over the set, that nothing would be ready for filming. I was running out of time to get the production in order.

One afternoon, panic set in. I called the head of production in the United States, Ronnie, and told him about the trouble. He said one sentence to me: "Before you go home tonight, find a man named Aria and tell him that Ronnie says hi." And I thought, *Oh yeah, that's going to help me?* Desperate, I ran around asking, "Is Aria here? Is Aria here?" Not one person would answer me. Then I came across a small cluster of men. I called out looking for Aria. Finally, from this dark huddle, one little face turned around but said nothing. So I said to him, "Ronnie told me to say hi." And with that he broke into this gigantic smile. He shook my hand and gave me a really big hug. I was baffled, thinking this must have been some secret message, some secret handshake. All I remember is that smile and his beautiful white teeth. After many weeks, it was the first moment of pure relief. Here was someone who wasn't going to give me a hard time. That was the beginning of our relationship.

I was staying in the nicest hotel in Tel Aviv, overlooking the Mediterranean. The night after Aria smiled at me, I asked him to come to the hotel and have dinner with me. Aria was the head of the art department and was building and designing everything for the film sets. Now, he's a construction kind of guy who was always in sweaty jeans, and he arrived at the hotel in what looked like his Bar Mitzvah suit from twenty years earlier. He couldn't speak much English, either, but somehow we managed to hit it off.

Aria explained what had really been going on. The fat man, Jacob, instructed the entire crew that if they talked to me, they would be fired. Jacob wanted me out so he could be the producer. I hadn't suspected any of this. Once the crew saw that Aria liked me, they started talking to me and working with me. Everything turned around.

One day Aria came over to my hotel so I could teach him how to play backgammon. He was lukewarm on the idea, so I told him suggestively, "If you play backgammon with me and win, you can do whatever you want! But if I win, I can do whatever

I want." Suddenly, he was totally into this game. He had no idea how to play, and I had to do everything in my power to let him win. That's how our love affair started.

From that moment on, I wasn't lonely anymore, I wasn't desperate. I wasn't unprotected. Just when you think the chips are down, suddenly everything can flip around and life can be the richest, fullest, and brightest. Things couldn't have been worse for me on this project and once I met Aria, that all changed.

I loved his generosity, his ability to be honest with me, his desire to make me really happy. It seemed like he was living just for me. He wanted to involve me in his life and to introduce me to people. He wanted to make me feel secure and protected. What was there not to fall in love with? In the beginning, I didn't know Aria was married or that he had children. I felt very guilty because he had a very nice wife. But it wasn't a question of who was nice and who wasn't. Our attraction was *all*-powerful and beyond logic or reason. It was a train going full steam and we were just the passengers.

I became so obsessed with Aria that I even lost interest in the production. The actors and directors were arriving soon in Israel, and I couldn't have cared less. It was so unlike me. We were both so neurotically, erotically in love that I couldn't function. We made love four times a day—in the car, in a restaurant, everywhere. It was constant, nonstop. Ours was an intense love like I had never experienced. Adding to the romance was the Mediterranean setting, which was gorgeous and exotic and new.

But Jacob was going insane. He fired Aria and called Aria's wife and told her what was going on. She came to confront me, and I repeatedly denied our affair. To cause even more trouble, Jacob hired my husband, Sam, as a director on one of my films in Israel. Sam called to say he was on his way to join me.

After Sam arrived, Aria and I continued to see each other. It's an inexplicable thing—on a film set, it's so easy to escape into a fantasy world. I thought at the time that Aria and I were experiencing something that I only read about in books. It almost seemed unreal.

Finally, everything in Israel was such a mess that I left and went back to New York, leaving both Aria and Sam behind. I thought that was the end of it.

After I returned to New York, I had to make a decision about divorcing Sam. Trying to sort through my confusion, I went to one of my close friends and asked for his advice. He told me that my husband had been involved with various men throughout our entire relationship.

My life flashed in front of me. Everything made sense when I learned the truth. It was very clear that I had to divorce Sam right away. We never had a big confrontation about any of this. He was a good person and he really did love me. I felt only compassion for him.

Simultaneously, I was offered a job in Los Angeles and I took it. Aria and I had been in touch with each other, and he had visited me once, though I had no fantasies about the future. But a few months after I arrived in L.A., Aria came back to me. He couldn't take it. He was too in love. I had no idea Aria would ever come to the United States and become my husband. I assumed that a passionate love affair this intense would eventually burn out. But our relationship evolved into so much more than that. Aria never moved back to Israel again.

After we divorced, Sam contracted HIV, and years later, he died of AIDS. I was never angry at Sam for putting me at risk. Instead, I only felt sorry for him. He really did love me and he truly was a good person, but had I stayed with him, I very well may have gotten sick, too. I like to think Aria saved my life. I must have said I wouldn't go to Israel a thousand times because it would change everything. It really was Aria who changed my life forever.

Kelly and Andrew

publications coordinator, 25; new media editor, 25,

married November 29, 1997

♥

My husband and I dated each other's *best* friends in college before we fell for each other. We became close confidants after I broke up with his friend Todd. Andrew had stopped seeing my friend Leslie not long before.

Andrew always intrigued me. He wore a long trench coat and had this crazy-looking winter scarf. Andrew was in more than one band throughout our college days, and was a deejay at the campus radio station. Even then, I think we liked each other, but we just didn't know it yet. For me, there were no hints. He did strike me, but in a curious way. I thought he was a great guy and a dependable friend and I'm sure he thought the same of me. We took classes together and would pass notes to each other like fifth graders during lectures. But that was all.

We were friends for about three years but had only been truly close for a few months when everything changed. One night when I was visiting him in his dorm, the power suddenly went out. The dorm corridors were the only places with any light, and all the students were jammed into the halls. When I found Andrew standing there, I gave him a hug and he never stopped holding me. Before I knew it, I was kissing him, and he was kissing me back. When the lights came back on, the guy he had been talking with next to him was a little stunned! It's amazing what a little power failure can do for romance.

We felt a little strange about the whole thing because we were our friends' exes. Among guy friends, dating another girl's ex is taboo, or at least a bad move if you want to hang on to that friend. Todd, my ex, who lived on the same floor in Andrew's dorm, found out about us pretty quickly. We were caught kissing in a rather obvious spot—lights or no lights—and word traveled fast. Todd was pretty upset and hasn't spoken to either of us since. I blamed myself about it for a long time and felt really guilty. My best friend Leslie, on the other hand, was actually a great supporter of the relationship. She thought we made a perfect couple, and I asked her to be one of my bridesmaids at our wedding.

I always tease Andrew that he sneaked into my heart by tricking me. Before Andrew, I had a very hard time committing to a relationship and tended to break things off as soon as it looked serious. Once Andrew and I agreed to date exclusively, which was a big deal, he actually bet me that I'd break up with him first. It was very smart of him. I'm a damned stubborn Irish girl, and I'd never let him be right about my reluctance to commit. I would *not* be the one to break up. So, I guess either the bet has gone too far, or Andrew just figured out the perfect way to keep me long enough for me to realize he was the one for me.

David and Wendy

doctor, 41; human resources executive, 33

married April 11, 1999

♥

When I finally met the right woman after years of searching, I nearly let her slip away from me. It was a very close call. I was on a singles ski trip in Snowmass, Colorado. The trip held the promise of two crucial elements: skiing, which I love, and the chance of meeting a woman, which I was very interested in after years of being alone. After the first day of skiing, there was a cocktail party for everyone on the trip—a meet-and-mingle sort of event. I was talking to a few people when I saw a woman across the room. I walked up to her and said hello.

Wendy was so much fun to talk to, that was the most important thing. She was also really cute and had a great smile, and was lively and energetic.

Soon the cocktail party was over, and the organizers were rounding everyone up for dinner. As Wendy and I walked over to the restaurant, suddenly, she peeled off with her friend Jill. I assumed we'd all be eating dinner together, but I realized that they weren't part of this singles' ski trip. They were crashers, and they'd been busted. To save money, Wendy and Jill decided to travel on their own instead of joining the organized trip, but they knew our itinerary because their friend Perry was a part of my group. I was a little disappointed when they told me good night, but we set a tentative time to meet on the mountain the next day for a little skiing.

I was so discouraged when I didn't find Wendy the next day. I was waiting at the designated spot on the mountain, but she and I missed each other. I had met a bunch of interesting women on this trip already, but Wendy was the one who really captivated me. She made me feel good just being around her.

The next day after skiing, I was walking down the hall to my hotel room when I passed a woman who said hello to me. I did a double take when I realized it was Wendy, standing there in her bathing suit—quite a switch from the sweater and jeans she was wearing when I first met her. I asked her if she wanted to join me in the hot tub. She said yes, even though it was pretty obvious she had already gone in once that night.

In the outdoor tub with the mountains surrounding us, such warm wonderful feelings flooded through me. It wasn't from the hot water; it was all about Wendy. She was so nice and kind and generous. She was so easy to be around, and I was very attracted to her. I wished everyone near us would have just disappeared. Out of nowhere, I thought to myself, *This is the girl I'm going to marry.* Ironically, our conversation wasn't the most romantic one in the world. Among other things, we discussed antibiotics and dental floss.

The final night of the trip there was a farewell party for the whole group. Since Wendy had shown up for so many of the events so far, I just assumed she'd be there. I searched and searched for Wendy, but she was nowhere to be found. Suddenly, it dawned on me that I might not see her again. My heart sank. I didn't have her phone number or any way of getting in touch with her. I didn't even know her last name. And since she wasn't on my trip, I wasn't able to track her down through the group directory. Then I remembered she was friends with one of the guys on my trip, Perry.

Once back home, I began my plotting. Searching through a list of all the skiers, I found Perry's address. I wrote a letter to Wendy and sent it in care of Perry, asking and hoping that he would get it to her. In my note I said that I hoped she might remember me: we had a hot tub conversation regarding the pros and cons of dental floss. I hovered tentatively over the mailbox with this letter in my hands and finally dropped it in. She called a few days later.

After I returned her to her apartment at the end of our first date, I felt so wonderful about the whole thing. Driving home that night, it dawned on me that Wendy was really the one. And I almost let her slip away. Not asking for her phone number after the hot tub night could have really cost me.

Wendy later told me that when she was planning her trip, her father really wanted her to take the singles trip instead of traveling on her own with Jill. He thought it would be a great idea for her to socialize with some available men. Wendy joked with her father, "Don't worry, Dad, I'll meet my husband, anyway." She was absolutely right.

Rita and John

teacher, 61; diplomat, 63
married May 27, 1972

♥

We met in the customs line at the airport, and by the time we reached baggage claim, my future husband had already asked me on our first date. It was 1970, and I was in Belgrade, the former Yugoslavia, visiting a friend and his family whom I tutored in English in New York City. After my stay in Yugoslavia, I was continuing on to Rome. But when I got to the airport in Belgrade, the airline was limiting who could and couldn't get on the plane. It turned out that then-head of the United Nations, U Thant, was on my flight, and lots of people were being bumped because of security concerns. It was an utter fluke that I was one of the dozen or so people who were cleared to board the plane. Coincidentally, I happened to know one of the Yugoslavian diplomats accompanying Thant because I tutored his daughter. He noticed me at the gate, introduced me to Thant, and got me through security. Little did I know that my future husband, John, was watching all of this activity from afar and was impressed that I was traveling among these high-powered officials. He was thinking, "Who is that woman?"

Because he's a diplomat, John was able to get on that plane to Rome as well. He hadn't planned to take that particular flight that day. He had been touring the coast of Yugoslavia with friends and, ready to leave, decided to take the first flight out of town. He didn't even care where he went, since he had some time to kill before returning to the United States. Luckily, that fateful flight to Rome was the first departure of the morning.

We didn't actually meet until we landed. John was standing in the customs line behind me when I asked him if he'd watch my luggage while I went to the restroom. While I was gone, he looked at my baggage tags and noticed that I lived on West Eighty-sixth Street in New York City. I later learned his parents lived on East Eighty-sixth Street!

John looked like a professor, with his baggy pants and horn-rimmed glasses. His salt-and-pepper hair was phenomenal—very full and gorgeous. And he was charming. I was impressed with his fluent Italian, which he demonstrated by talking to people all over the Rome airport. It was while we were waiting for our luggage to come down the baggage carousel that he asked me to have dinner with him that night. I knew that because of his excellent Italian, we'd at least eat well! I accepted his invitation since I had no plans and didn't know anyone in town.

We went to a great little trattoria that night, and I was bowled over by him. He had lived in Italy for several years as a Fulbright scholar, and I was quite impressed. He had studied Italian history as a Ph.D. student and then later joined the Foreign Service. In Rome, John was on terra firma and really took charge. He seemed very straightforward and sincere. There was no nonsense about him. John was great fun to be with and was so intelligent. I liked his directness, and I was amazed by all of the things he had accomplished.

We spent a marvelous week together in Rome. John showed me all around the city—the ruins, the sights and hidden trattorias. At the end of the week, he suggested we go to a wonderful little island off the coast called Julio. We had a great time on this beautiful island, and it was obvious we were both interested in each other. Our romantic weekend there was one I'll never forget.

When I returned home to New York, I wasn't sure what would come of this European affair. Our romance had developed very quickly and who knew—maybe once we returned to our regular lives that would be the end of it. But John called me as soon as he was back in Washington, and he visited me in New York that very weekend. By the fourth weekend, he took me to meet his father and stepmother on East Eighty-sixth Street. Evidently, John brought his dirty laundry with him every time he came to the city, and his stepmother would wash it. Much to my surprise, she presented me with a bag filled with his clean socks and underwear as soon as I arrived. She assumed I'd be taking over this job now. I took it as a pretty good sign that John and I were going to stay together. Even his parents could tell we were meant to be.

Claudia and Gordon

human resources executive, 33; advertising executive, 33
married September 19, 1992

♥

I met my husband at a city bus stop. We had seen each other there before and acknowledged each other with a nodding glance. But one day after work, he just walked up to me and said hello while we were waiting on the sidewalk. We talked the whole way home and realized that we lived in the same area and worked not only in the same building, but also for the same company. As I got off the bus he said something about calling me sometime, and I told him I'd like that.

Gordon likes to deny it, but two days later, I was across the hall from my office and out of the corner of my eye I saw someone snooping around my desk. He was in there scoping out my office, and I *totally* busted him! Gordon worked on the twenty-ninth floor and I on the eighth. He had absolutely no reason to come downstairs other than to see me. I knew he was interested.

He was cute and really nice, but I didn't know much about

him. Of course, I was asking around at work about him. A few nights later he called and invited me to a formal charity event.

My roommates and I had just been moaning about how we couldn't meet any nice guys and we weren't invited to any formal Christmas parties. We were so annoyed. After Gordon called, I strutted around the apartment, giving my poor friends a hard time. I was making a huge deal about it: I bought a new dress, new shoes, and got a manicure the day before. But when the day of the party arrived, I woke up and I was so sick, I couldn't even get out of bed. I was lying in bed thinking I was going to die. But I still *really* wanted to go to the party. At 3:00 P.M. I thought I'd finally have to call Gordon and cancel. But my roommate told me to take her cold medicine. "It's the greatest stuff in the world," she said. So I gave it a try and it helped. I still felt pretty bad, but I got ready for the evening, thinking I could muddle through. Right before Gordon picked me up, I took another two doses of the medicine as a precautionary measure.

Gordon was having preparty cocktails at his house for his friends. I was all dressed up, and he was in a tux and looked great. I ended up drinking some wine and talking to Gordon's best friend for a while. The friend asked me some basic question like what year I graduated, and I just sat there, dumbfounded, unable to speak. I couldn't get a word out. I slipped off the bar stool and stumbled down the hall, where I walked right into a wall and almost fell down. When Gordon came over to ask me if I was all right, I didn't tell him I had overdosed on cold medicine! I made it into the bathroom just before I started throwing up like a maniac. I was *so* sick. My eyes rolled back, I was drooling, and I practically passed out. I think I was in there for a half an hour—who knows?—when this girl dragged me back out to the party. All of the guys were saying, "Nice date, Gordon!" assuming, I'm sure, that I was completely loaded. When they sat me down on the couch, I literally toppled over and passed out immediately. They left me lying there on the couch for an hour and a half while the party was going on around me.

When I woke up later, I felt completely fine. I ate something and we went to the party and had a blast the rest of the night. Of course, when I went home that night I read the cold medicine box, and it said DO NOT MIX WITH ALCOHOL!

I thought Gordon was cute, but a different kind of cute than the guys I normally liked. But he was really nice. Just a sweet, sweet guy. What really touched me was that even after I barfed in his bathroom, passed out at his party, and embarrassed him in front of all his friends, he called me the next day and wanted to see me again. After only a few weeks, I was hooked and told my roommates that I was going to marry this guy. You just never know who you might find on the bus ride home.

Corey and Amy

real estate developer, 43; mother and teacher, 39

married June 23, 1990

♥

$\mathcal{I}$n a way, you could say ours is an arranged marriage. Amy and I were set up by, of all people, her father.

I knew Amy's dad because we played golf together at the same club. Once, he asked if I might be interested in taking out his daughter and I said okay, just to be polite. However I was getting a little sick of the blind-date circuit. Soon afterward, Amy started seeing someone, and when her father told me about this recent development, I was relieved.

But six months later she was available again, and once more her father floated the blind-date idea. Since I had already said yes the first time around, I couldn't see any nice way of getting out of it, even though I was less than enthusiastic.

The night we were to have dinner, the Knicks were playing in a big playoff game. I was pretty disappointed that I had to turn off this exciting game to pick up this girl whom I had no desire to get involved with. I postponed leaving my apartment as long as I could. I kept looking at my watch, knowing I was going to be really late. There were still two minutes left in the game when I made myself leave, and the Knicks were down by ten or twelve points. I was sure they'd lose and I wouldn't miss anything.

When I saw Amy for the very first time, she was wearing a winter white outfit and a belt with a Mickey Mouse buckle. I rolled my eyes thinking, *Boy, this is going to be a great night.* I, on the other hand, was wearing a very sharp shirt and tie combo that I was quite proud of. Amy later told me she and her mother analyzed my clothes and decided my outfit was the dumbest thing they'd ever seen. But her mother made a strong push for me. "Forget the outfit," she'd said. "Focus on his dimples."

The evening was uneventful. While we were getting the check, though, out of the blue Amy said, "You know, the Knicks won tonight in overtime." I couldn't believe it! My first thought *I'd missed the end of a great game,* but then it dawned on me, *Wait a minute, she knows about sports. She's a Knicks fan!* It was a huge moment, a turning point in our fledging relationship. In all honesty, this one little comment was a big part of why I asked her for a second date. If she hadn't mentioned the Knicks, I might not have been inspired to see her again.

The fact that she then invited me to a Mets game made me think that we really might have something in common. And then there was the quirky coincidence that her last name was the same as a famous baseball player whose card was the most valuable one in my collection. I started to think that maybe the gods were trying to tell me something here. Maybe it was fate.

Even though with us it wasn't love at first sight, the fact that she was a real sports fanatic kept things going long enough for our romance to take off and for us to fall in love with each other.

Very early on, I really had no expectations that something lasting was going to come of Amy and me. And when you don't burden yourself with all those expectations and pressure, that's when things just happen naturally.

Our relationship bloomed slowly at first. We were just dating and enjoying each other's company for the first few months. We found each other very interesting and had so many common passions, like kids and travel. Amy was—and still is—very outgoing. I love that spunk of hers. I, on the other hand, am more reserved. We really seemed to work together as a couple.

One day about six months after we met, I told Amy, "My God, I'm falling in love with you." The realization just came over me suddenly out of the blue. It was like doing a puzzle. I put the pieces together and started to visualize what the puzzle was going to look like. I thought, *There is something different about the way I feel for Amy. This could go pretty far.* And a month later, I proposed to her.

Now, I tell my unmarried friends that if lightning doesn't strike on a first date, don't give up. One friend of mine expects fireworks to go off immediately. But the real world just isn't always like that. Look at Amy and me. Had Amy not made that offhand comment and I hadn't asked her on a second date, I would have missed out on a lifetime with the woman I love. We got our fireworks. We just had to be a little patient.

Mirion and Geraldine

surgeon, 64; grandmother, 60-something

married June 21, 1956

❤

Mirion: It was *total* entrapment. During college at Florida A & M, one of the many jobs I had was working in the library. I was in periodicals, dealing with fifty- or sixty-year-old papers. So this lady here—

Geraldine: Now don't get so dramatic.

Mirion: I was about fifteen years old.

Geraldine: Oh, you were not.

Mirion: I was a child prodigy.

Geraldine: And I'm this old woman?

Mirion: I thought I was telling this story! Anyway, Gerry came into the library because she was working on a research paper. She'd ask for these *old* magazines which I had to dig up all the way down in the dungeon of the library. And she just kept coming, every day.

Geraldine: I was doing my term paper on "To Spank or Not to Spank Children." I got an A, too.

Mirion: After the term was over and the next semester rolled around, Gerry came back to the library every day and kept requesting the old newspapers from me.

Geraldine: You're exaggerating. When I finished my term paper, that was it!

Mirion: No, she kept asking me for help. And I *really* got tired of going downstairs and getting all that research—

Geraldine: Now you know I didn't come back to that library after the term was over.

Mirion: Finally, I thought, *I've got to figure some way to not have to go downstairs anymore.* It was really hard work. Those old magazines were really dusty. So I asked her out for a date.

Geraldine: I think I said, "No, I don't have time. I have to study."

Mirion: No, she said, "Oh, yes! I was wondering when you were going to ask me!"

Geraldine: I will tell you, this probably sounds snobbish or whatever. But I just couldn't see even dating someone who was not alert. Mirion was alert. There were a lot of guys who *adored* me. Handsome ones. There was one who was really nice, but he couldn't read. It had been instilled in me that intellect begets intellect. And I didn't want to have any dumb kids. And Mirion has these beautiful light brown eyes. . . .

Mirion: There was only one place to go out that night of our first date: the Sweet Shop.

Geraldine: No, no. You're thinking of the Fountainette.

Mirion: Yes! The Fountainette! They had a jukebox. And you could have milk shakes.

Geraldine: Let me tell you something, when homeboy here came out and discovered the Fountainette, you would have thought he found the Fountain of Youth. "Golly! Look at this!" he said.

Mirion: All I remember is having to go get those papers. And that after I asked Gerry out and we started dating, her research was over. No more digging through the basement for me.

Cynthia and Ron

accessory designer, 42; custom jewelry manufacturer, 44

married October 3, 1993

♥

I collided with my future husband on Sunday, February 2, at the Twenty-sixth Street flea market in New York. It was eighteen degrees out, and Ron was on his bicycle. I was leaving the market when we literally bumped smack into each other. His face looked familiar.

We had met each other twenty years earlier, in high school. We were both from Brooklyn but had gone to different schools and barely knew each other. Over the years he'd become incredibly handsome with his dark skin and gorgeous salt-and-pepper hair. During our encounter at the market, it struck me that Ron was such a kind, warm, genuine human being that it was an immediate turn-on. I remember that day like it was yesterday.

That day I felt a closeness with him because of our shared background, a comfort level that you don't get very often. Leaving the flea market, we went for cappuccino. By the second cup, I knew. I had this feeling this was a person who was going to be in my life forever. I was just absolutely sure he was the right man for me. Not only was I attracted to him sexually, but I could also picture him as a solid family man.

At one point I was going to say good-bye to go to my exercise class, but he instead suggested we go work out together at his gym. After the workout, we looked at each other and said simultaneously, "Sushi?" Then we were off to the movies. It was just euphoria. I was so happy and energetic, I didn't know what to do with myself. We were still together after midnight. We ended up going to a club in the East Village to listen to music, and we started passionately kissing in the middle of the bar. I just didn't want the night to ever end.

I can recount everything that happened in the first year of our relationship. We sent each other invitations for special dinners and everything he did was very romantic. We went on so many little weekend trips to quaint little places like Montreal, Sag Harbor, Shelter Island, and Martha's Vineyard.

I knew this time was something special that I'd want to remember forever, so I created a big collage scrapbook of our first year together. In it I pasted a collection of memorabilia of everything we did. I saved every movie stub, matchbooks from jazz clubs we went to, romantic postcards he sent me, and playbills from every play we saw. I saved all of the things I knew would become nostalgic to us in later years. It's very special.

Ron and I have similar taste. We like the same music, we like the same furniture, and we like the same places. With Ron, it was like I was in a car and I had a destination, and nothing could stop me from getting to where I was going. But I didn't plan it like that. I just knew it was right. For a relationship to work for me, has to be easy and effortless.

I tell my single friends, there are three A's of dating: No analyzing, no assuming, and no anticipating. Those are the rules I lived by. I didn't play games, I just tried to be myself. You wait your whole life for the right person to come along. I knew someday I'd find a man who would appreciate me just as I was. And Ron was that somebody.

Valri and Bob

advertising salesperson, 41; actor, 38

married August 2, 1991

♥

Many years ago, my best friend, Anne, and I went to see the movie *Beaches*. Her husband, Bob, had *insisted* that we go. He just thought it was the most wonderful movie. Well, we walked out of there laughing about how corny and unbelievable it was! The idea that one friend dies and the other takes over her children was just so old-fashioned Hollywood. I remembered this day many years later and thought how ironic it was that I became the mother of Anne's three girls.

Anne and I were friends as teenagers, and we'd reconnected as adults, in Los Angeles. She was married to someone else we'd known when we were younger, a man named Bob. Eventually my husband and I split up, and it was Bob and Anne who really helped me through that difficult time. While I was gathering myself together, I moved into Bob and Anne's guest house. They had a little girl, Amanda, whom I adored. Not long after Amanda was born, Anne found out she was pregnant again—with twins! She was a very petite woman, not quite five feet tall, and had a very difficult pregnancy. My plan was to stay with her until after she delivered, then go to Europe for a few months. Another relationship had just ended for me and I needed to "dump my purse," organize my life, and just start over.

The twin girls were born prematurely. They were going to be okay, but they had to stay in the hospital for a good long while. Before Anne and Bob even brought them home, Anne's neck started to swell up dramatically. Her doctors discovered it was an aneurysm, and she needed surgery to remove it. The day of the surgery, I was taking care of Amanda while Bob waited at the hospital. As time went on and on, I started getting more and more worried. No one at the hospital would tell me how she was doing because I wasn't immediate family, which only made me more concerned. Finally Bob's mother called me and told me that Anne had died on the operating table. She was only thirty years old.

We were devastated. When Bob came home that night and we looked at each other, I just knew that this family was going to be a really big part of my life in some way. Whatever my future held, this man and these children were going to be an extension of my family. Bob was only twenty-nine years old and had an eighteen-month-old daughter and two infants. He needed help desperately. I canceled my trip and devoted myself to taking care of Anne's babies.

She was my very best friend and had such an incredible influence on my life. Her death was devastating for me and is still the most difficult loss I've ever experienced. It was the most dramatic, pivotal turning point in my life. Nothing would ever be the same again. Even now, almost ten years later, I don't go a day in my life without thinking about Anne.

Bob and I did our best to take care of the babies. We were both working, but during evenings and weekends, We took care of the girls. We had bottles for three, diapers for three. It was a huge responsibility, but somehow we made it work. The funny thing was that Anne once told me she didn't think I should have children. I was too independent, she thought!

Bob and I were united by these babies. The drama of Anne's death—not to mention our love for these three beautiful girls—created such an emotional bond. There was a closeness that began growing between us, and the things that Anne had always loved about Bob I now saw in him much more vividly—his joy for life, devotion to his family, his humility, and his willingness to always see the best in people. It was very difficult not to like and respect Bob. I was having a very difficult time not falling in love with him.

During the first year after Anne was gone, I had to go on a business trip to Las Vegas, and knowing that Bob desperately needed a break from work and children, I asked him to come along. I had absolutely no romantic intentions and just thought it would be a good opportunity for him to relax and have some fun for the first time in a very long while. It was in Las Vegas that things began to shift between us. We talked for hours and hours. We took long walks and started opening ourselves up to each other on a much more intimate level. We had been relying on each other so much over the last months, and suddenly, our vision of the future changed directions entirely. The possibility of our being together as a couple to complete this family seemed to burst out of nowhere.

It wasn't until months later, though, that Bob surprised me one day. He told me simply that he was falling in love with me and we had to decide what to do about it. I was falling in love with him, too, but was scared to death. The stakes were very high, and there was no playing around. I couldn't continue to mother the girls and to live with Bob day in and day out if we weren't going to make a very serious commitment to each other. And if we weren't, I needed to move out because I didn't want to get too attached to the girls. More important, I didn't want the girls to get too close to me and then lose another significant woman in their lives.

I had dreams about Anne all the time. In some of them, she was irritated about my being with Bob. In others, she was very happy about it. For a long time I felt that it was just too odd and that I was overstepping the boundaries of my friendship with her. I had many a tearful night. But there are rules about this kind of situation. I asked Bob if he ever felt guilty about loving me and he said no. Anne was a great love of his life. But she was gone, and he felt that we were all bundled together for a reason. I also knew it was right and that Bob and I, along with Anne's children, could make a very happy family.

Anne is still a very important part of our lives. I believe that she's aware of where we all are now and is happy for us. When I look back over the many years since she died, I see that there was really a place for me in this family. I was Anne's best friend and I tell her children about what a wonderful woman she was. These girls know all about the woman they call her their first mommy. I think Anne would be really happy.

When I was my younger, independent self, I never saw a sub-urban life in my future. It was so unattractive to me. Now, the most fun I can think of is sitting with my girls and my husband watching kids' Friday night TV or doing Girl Scout projects. They are my life. Every once in a while, I miss what I used to have, but nothing would be worth trading my family.

I know I was in Anne's life for a reason. Anne's death was tragic and unexpected, but it was god-sent that I was able to carry on her legacy and live the life that she couldn't. She and Bob and the girls have fulfilled my life in ways that I never even dreamed of.

Shelly and David

advertising executive, 37; lawyer, 43

married September 21, 1996

♥

I have my hairdresser to thank for my marriage.

I was thirty years old and had just broken up with my boyfriend when I went in for my usual haircut with Vallerium, a beautiful, wonderful, flamboyant Brazilian hairstylist who's relatively famous in Portland. Like many women, I have a very good relationship with my hairdresser.

While he's cutting—or *designing*, as they say—Vallerium and I were chatting away. He knew that I had just gotten out of a relationship, and he was very sympathetic. Suddenly, in walked Michael, a friend of Vallerium's. Michael is a key figure in this tale of love and matchmaking.

Vallerium introduced me to Michael and felt the need to mention to him that I was newly single. "Michael," he said, "You're always good at matching people." Michael launched into full "Yenta" mode and decided he was going to find me a man! Now,

Michael is an effusive sort of character. He whipped out a pad of paper and started asking me questions about my ideal mate. I was trapped in the chair, and I remember thinking, *What the hell, I have nothing to lose.* I was very interested in meeting someone and willing to try anything. Michael was furiously jotting down notes. "What should he look like?" he asked. "What type of personality do you prefer? Professionally, what's good for you?" And I was just spewing out information.

"I like them tall and thin," I told him. "Basketball bodies are better. Careerwise, no more advertising people. I've had enough! How about an architect? He would have a balance of both creative and technical qualities. I don't care if he has kids, but no baggage, if you please. He has to respect my love of travel, even if he doesn't share my passion for it."

I was unabashedly enthusiastic about this silly project. I was pretty loud and it turned into *such* a scene. Michael was carrying on. Vallerium was carrying on. We were all causing quite a commotion flapping our gums about my ideal man. I wasn't noticing or caring that the entire salon was listening in on this crazy conversation.

At one point, Michael said, "I have to tell these men something about you. Let's see, you're tall, *relatively* attractive . . ." *Thanks a lot, pal,* I thought! Other things I added to my list were that I worked in advertising and loved to travel. Michael noticed that I didn't sound like I was from the West Coast, and I told him I'm a Midwesterner. "Me too," said Michael, "Where are you from?" "Wisconsin," I answered. To which Michael said, "I'm from Wisconsin, too. Antigo." I freaked out! "Michael," I told him, "I'm from *Wausau!*" These are two little Wisconsin towns, only miles apart. Suddenly, the guy sitting in the chair next to me—who I had not even slightly noticed, who had not said a *word* the entire time—leaned over and inserted himself into our conversation. Casually, he announced, "I'm from Steven's Point." That's right near where I grew up!

For the next few minutes, we had this bizarre, central Wisconsin small-town reunion. "Do you have family there?" I asked. "Going home for the holidays?" he wanted to know. "What high school did you go to?" Michael asked. We had a moment of reminiscing and fun, and then it broke up.

Back underneath Vallerium's scissors, I thought fleetingly, *Hmm, the Steven's Point guy is pretty cute.* Michael and I then finished up our interview. Since it was Christmastime, he told me it might take a while for him to get to work on this. But he promised me, "I've got people."

As I was paying for my haircut, I noticed that someone was staring at me in one of the mirrors. It was the man from Steven's Point. Hey, I'm no fool. I wasn't about to pass up such an opportunity. I walked up to him, touched him on the shoulder, and wished him a wonderful Christmas in Wisconsin. He wished me a happy holidays, too, and then added, "You know, your haircut, it looks *fine*." Fine? I thought that was a pretty odd thing to say. I walked out of there thinking the guy from the chair told me I have so-so hair and Michael classified me as relatively attractive. It wasn't a great self-esteem moment.

A few weeks later, I went back to the salon for some highlighting. Vallerium was booming with energy, saying, "Oh, Shelly! Didn't we have *so* much fun a couple of weeks ago! *Everybody* was talking about it. Michael can't wait to set you up, and we're all rooting for you!" Then he casually said, "Hey, what about the guy in the chair next to you?" I had almost no opinion about this guy in the chair—he was wearing a cape, his hair was wet, and I hardly even got a good look at him. I had no idea if he was straight, single, or interested. Refusing to let it go, Vallerium asked me if I wanted him to do a little snooping to find out who he was.

Vallerium told me to leave one of my business cards with him so that the next time this guy came into the salon, he could casually hand it to him. So I figured what the hell and left my card. I hated blind dates, but this was infinitely better than meeting someone in a bar.

By the end of January, I still hadn't heard from Michael and had put the whole thing out of my mind. Off on a business trip one day, I called into the office for messages and my secretary told me that a man named David from the city attorney's office called and that Vallerium referred him to me. Oh God, it was one of Michael's setups! *What have I done?* I thought in a panic. I didn't have the energy for an awkward date with a stranger.

But Michael had clearly gone out of his way to set up this introduction, and I had to return the message. So I called up this David a few days later. On the phone, he sounded really nervous, in a very cute and endearing way. Before I could get any information about him, he said, "Thank you for leaving your business card." *Oh no! It's the guy in the chair!* I was wracking my brains, trying to remember what he looked like and how old he might have been. I hardly remembered him. The conversation became even more awkward and nerve-racking. Never before had I just passed out my card like that. It was pretty bold of me. So in an attempt to end the conversation and just get off the phone, I said, "Listen David, I'm a little nervous about this, but thank you for calling." He wasn't about to let me go and said, "Hey, hey, hey! Don't worry about it. I'm really glad you put the onus on the hair salon. Obviously, you didn't see my ad."

Ad? He took out an ad? My entire mood changed, and, instinctively, I branded him as some sort of wild freak! I asked him, "What ad? Where was it?" It ran in the alternative newspaper with all the personals in the back under Chance Meetings, he told me. I was sure that this ad was horrid and read something like, "Hey, met you in the hair salon. Nice tits. Please call." David was very smooth about it all. He said to me, "You left your card looking for me. I took out an ad looking for you—the least we can do is have lunch." *Well, good for him,* I thought, *for cutting right to the chase.* I agreed to meet on one condition: that he bring the ad.

I was put off about the existence of this personal ad before I saw it. It would be really telling about his personality if it was desperate, sexual, or stupid. When I saw it at lunch the next day, I realized it was none of the above. It read, "Antigo, how can I get onto Wausau's list? Signed, Steven's Point." If I had seen that in the paper, I would have been the only woman in the world to get it. I was terribly impressed. It was a clever intellectual puzzle, and it was intimate. You never think someone's taking out an ad looking for *you.*

He was cute, really cute. But the only thing I knew about him was that he was from Steven's Point. It felt very much like a blind date, with all the attending nerves and anxiety. I don't care what anyone says, blind dates don't get any easier. He could have turned out to be some schlep. But instead he seemed intriguing. He was a rock climber and a pilot and did all kinds of interesting things. David is smart and terribly funny. We realized right away that we are the exact opposites. He is very cerebral, very intellectual, very book smart. As a lawyer, he is a man of order and rules and he speaks no more than he has to. I, on the other hand, am a woman of emotions. I'm talkative, expressive, and social. We are 180 degrees apart. Had we met a few years earlier, we would never have never been interested in each other. It took some maturity for us each to recognize that we could love and appreciate someone so different from ourselves.

I wanted to give myself the opportunity to get to know him because I was really intrigued. When I thought about how he had tried to track me down, I found it all so very sweet and touching. It was such a kind gesture. My polite David didn't want to involve the hair salon in his search for me and to this day, he apologizes to them about it all. Vallerium, on the other hand, has been bragging about his matchmaking ever since.

We've told our sweet story seven hundred times. The way we met was so much better than if someone had tried to set me up with some lawyer from the city attorney's office. That little bit of drama that unfolded made everything so much more exciting. It was exactly how we should have met.

About the Authors

♥

Michelle Bowers is a San Francisco–based freelance writer whose work has been published in *Entertainment Weekly*, *Shape*, *People*, *Parenting*, and *Health* magazines.

Melissa Steinfeld Galett is an executive recruiter in magazine publishing who lives and works in New York City.

We'd love to hear about how you met your spouse. If you'd like to send us your story, please contact us at: michellebowers@sprintmail.com.